Crossing Borders
A Hispanic Experience

Jan H. Oller

Bloomington, IN  Milton Keynes, UK

AuthorHouse™
1663 Liberty Drive, Suite 200
Bloomington, IN 47403
www.authorhouse.com
Phone: 1-800-839-8640

AuthorHouse™ UK Ltd.
500 Avebury Boulevard
Central Milton Keynes, MK9 2BE
www.authorhouse.co.uk
Phone: 08001974150

First published by AuthorHouse 5/1/2006

ISBN: 1-4259-1744-5 (sc)

Printed in the United States of America
Bloomington, Indiana

This book is printed on acid-free paper.

First and foremost this book is dedicated to all those who made it possible. To all of those who have ever found themselves in the position of crossing borders, both literal and metaphorical, searching for something new, something better, yet found themselves in a world where the only thing they ended up searching for was themselves. To those who realize that in today's world, to seek and speak the truth is in itself a revolutionary act.

TABLE OF CONTENTS

CHAPTER 1

Preliminary Contemplations

"The United States is a unique case in history, an imperialism in search of universality."
- Octavio Paz

"Once you see yourself truthfully depicted, you have a sense of your right to be in the world"

- Paul Marshall

1.0 An introduction to the work and the processes involved in its creation.

Upon setting out to conduct my research, it was my intent to simply gain an understanding of my consultants, to transcribe their stories within a theoretical framework that best serves to expand the current body of knowledge of language and identity among transnational groups. Person centered interviewing techniques were used to the extent that the consultant was viewed as a knowledgeable person able to teach me about the culture and behavior of their particular group. It was my intent to view the consultants not merely as "informants" or as "test subjects" but to gain an understanding of them as people, as individuals, to see their human qualities without judging them but rather embracing their experience and attempting to understand it. The use of open ended, purposely ambiguous probes allowed me to accomplish this, an emphasis on the contents and forms of responses were seen as providing important material for analysis. The interviews were conducted over a span of 3 months, in informal social situations, with the place of interview ranging from restaurants, to the homes of the consultants. The results of these interviews were affected not only by the approach which I chose, but also by the ethnicity, class, gender, education level, religious affiliation, political leanings, and age of the consultants as well. It must further be noted that the consultants are not merely the product of the cultures of their nations of origin, and to an extent American culture, but that they are also individuals, and thus the notion of agency cannot be avoided when assessing the research results. It is for this reason that the consultants cannot be taken to represent the Hispanic community of the United States per se, but rather represent diverse aspects of the Hispanic experience, which in turn is but an aspect of the human experience.

1.1 Methods to be used and their complexities concerning the importance of language and the ability to communicate and validate a world view. The ability to understand the "other."

In connection with the person-centered interviews, observations of the Hispanic community in Las Vegas were made. The areas observed were those where a highly concentrated Hispanic population resides, namely the area between Las Vegas Boulevard and I 15, and Sahara Avenue and Charleston Boulevard, commonly known as Meadows Village as well as the area between Bonanza Road and Owens Avenue, and the stretch along 28th Street and Bruce Avenue, an area also referred to as "Little Mexico." The observations consisted of participating in daily life in these predominantly Hispanic areas, patronizing the local business, engaging in local nightlife, cultural events, situations which not only put me in the position to interact with the local population but also to experience what they experience, to step into their world rather than merely look at it from afar. Without sufficient knowledge of the Spanish language, this would have been impossible, as when one views any culture, it is impossible to gain a full and comprehensive understanding as well as an appreciation for it without being able to fully communicate with the people one wishes to study. Language is the vehicle through which culture itself is communicated, and its comprehension allows one to not only understand others, but to understand how they perceive the world. For example, the Spanish phrase for "how old are you?" would translate as "¿Cuántos años tienes?" The Spanish translation is literally "how many years do you have?" thus showing a completely different view of age, while in the English speaking world view, age is something a person is, a state of being, of becoming, in the Spanish speaking world the same concept is transmitted in terms of having, owning, age is something one has, one acquires. Such a simple phrase conveys an immensely different world view when one examines it, for this reason, it is imperative that one understands those they observe, as well as their consultants as when translation occurs, certain meanings and understanding are sure to be lost. Within this context, language takes on the meaning of a complex semiotic system relying not merely on verbal communication but also on the most diverse forms of media, the plastic arts, graphics, dance, music, and poetry. In effect it represents the entire repertoire used to communicate the world view of a specific culture.

1.2 Determinants of the use of Spanish vs. English while conducting fieldwork.

During my observations, and the interviews as well, the use of the Spanish or English languages was determined by those I interacted with as well as by my consultants. Whichever they would begin the interaction with, or would switch to would be the one I used as well. The purpose of this was to allow for a natural flow of communication and expression, as well as for the comfort of those I was engaged with. Another reason was to track the role the Spanish language has in their lives, the context where it is used to communicate, and the circumstances in which it serves as a comfort zone. To determine the extent to which it serves as a political language for some, or as a means of everyday communication for others.

1.3 The role of literary research and theory in my work. The general organization of my work and my research philosophy, to approach the project without preconceived notions regarding the results.

The last portion of my research consisted of reviewing literature concerning similar investigations, as no literature dealing with exactly the same topic has been written to date. The purpose of this procedure was to be able to contemplate and create a theoretical model into which to place the collected data. To create a theoretical model which could be applied to the study of any situation where a history of migration and asymmetrical power relationships in constant flux between two or more groups, or geopolitical entities exists. While allowing for a focus on the commonly ignored features of language, pan-identity, and historical antecedence within this specific context. While organizing my research into this work, I decided to place this portion of my research first, and to allow a natural flow of events as I trace the processes involved in identity formation, and express the relevance of my theoretical model in the realms of theory, the general situation of Hispanics in the United States, and the Mexican transnational population in the United States. I then present the second portion of my work, which involves the application of my theoretical model on a local level with a first of its kind approach to the Mexican transnational populace of Las Vegas, Nevada. In order to avoid as much bias as possible, I attempted to enter the research without any notions of a preconceived outcome. Notions of success and failure arise when one has a preconceived goal in mind, within that context, failure or success is determined by how closely one's findings match their views of how things could or should be rather than the way they are. Instead, I chose an analytical approach which focuses on reporting what is, what my research has yielded. Rather than viewing myself as an experimenter, I view myself as an interpreter, with my immediate task being to interpret the world of my observations and my consultants, a world which exists rather than one which could be, should be, or was, with my sole goal being to bring to light the experience of the world of those I had the privilege of coming into contact with. In these terms, success and failure rest merely on the implication of whether my research gives an adequate voice to my consultants and their experience.

PART I.

Globalizing Currents and Identity:
Reflections on Becoming,
the Creation of a Theoretical Model

CHAPTER 2
The Self and the Other, Reflecting on Literary Antecedents

2.0 A deconstruction of writing methods, notes on the importance of position in literature.

When conducting any research, or viewing that of others, it is important to first consider one's own position as well as that taken by the authors of one's sources. Researcher bias cannot be ignored as attempted predictions of behavior tend to resemble the researcher's own ideological paradigms concerning human societies and the world around them. Thus saying something about the other may imply more about oneself and one's own world view than that of those they attempt to study. When dealing with societies which do not belong to the western, industrial, "first world" it becomes difficult, if not nearly impossible for the Westerner to fully comprehend a non-western, non-industrial world view due to the West's very own ideological blindfold. After a life of juxtaposing the values of Western industrial societies over non-Western, non-industrial contexts, of naturalizing power to the point that the capitalist notions of "competition for material gain" and a "social hierarchy based on materialism" are juxtaposed over the animal kingdom and even the most remote ages of human evolution, one becomes unable to escape the hegemonic constructs which have so heavily been internalized.

2.1 Discourse as power and the power of discourse. Ritual and the power of exclusion, the pliability of hegemony.

In this sense, discourse becomes power itself as it allows for the defining of truth through a system of domination and exclusion. People are limited as to what thoughts they may express through language as ideas are restricted by the boundaries of discourse, with discourse not being just a body of language but rather a body of language formed in a specific moment. Once it is created, discourse excludes ideas it does not favor. It is this very ability to exclude and reject ideas which allows for it to shape thought, and ultimately the nature of truth. While truth itself becomes a construct of power as it exercises a power of constraint upon other forms of discourse(Foucault, 1983). Something can only be said if it is positioned within a form of discourse, the enunciation is always from some subject who is positioned by and in discourse(Hall, 1990). External definition processes imply the imposition of a putative name and characterization by one set of actors upon another, affecting in significant ways the social experience of the categorized(Jenkins, 2003).

Among the most pertinent exclusionary forces in discourse is ritual, as s set of rules and dogma which restrict what can be said and by whom within a discipline. In religion, politics, and even science, ritual is based on paradigms one must adhere to in order to have a sense of credibility, as truth, morality, and meaning are created through discourse. It serves as the paradigm within which the world is interpreted. This notion allows for the exclusion and rejection not only of ideas, but of individuals because they fall outside the borders of accepted discourse. Yet change is possible as long as one possesses the ability of language, of communication, as it allows for the formation of counter-discursive elements, and their dispersal(Foucault, 1983). However, it must also be brought to mind that hegemony is never completed; it is always in a constant rush to enclose more differences within itself so as to ascertain that the projects of its individuals are only possible within the constraints of its cover(Hall, 1991). Hegemony is pliable in that it will appropriate and remodel ideas viewed as problematic to itself so as to create the illusion that nothing is possible unless it occurs under hegemony's umbrella.

2.2 The deterritorialization of space and its relevance to identity formation. The realm of imagination as empowering within anti-colonial/anti-globalizing discourse.

Until rather recently, and even to a certain extent today, the discourse of officialdom has failed to address, and still does not adequately address the effects of colonialism, and its subsequent offspring, globalization, on the cultures and peoples of the post-colonial world. Anthropology has always acknowledged the experience of space as being a social construct, yet has expressed little self consciousness about the very issue of space. It is assumed to be defined merely by breaks, ruptures, and disjunctions, and societies and individuals are believed to be merely occupying "naturally discontinuous" space. A concept so ingrained in Western culture that the world takes on the image of a collection of countries, divided into various national societies, with each being deeply rooted in what is seen as its proper place. A look on any map, or globe attests to this common construction of categorizing the world. Yet the notion of "Postmodern hyperspace," a phrase coined by Jameson in 1984, has challenged the very construct of mapping culture onto places and people(Gupta, 1992). Thus alluding to the fact that transnationalism has resulted in the creation of space through the reworking of ideas of home and community within the spheres of memory and imagination. Such a theoretical approach allows for an examination of the disjuncture of space and culture, and the formulation of various ways of dealing with cultural difference while abandoning preconceived notions of localized culture. The deterritorialization of space allows us to fundamentally reconceptualize the very politics of community, identity, solidarity, and cultural difference as identity does not rest specifically on an appropriation of physical space(Gupta, 1992). Identities are becoming less and less fixed as the mobility of people and cultural products, refugees, migrants, the stateless and displaced peoples of the world create what Edward Said has referred to as "a generalized condition of homelessness." Hence we encounter a situation where the notions of here and there, center and periphery, colony and metropole, become blurred(Gupta, 1992). Rather, remembered places serve as the symbolic anchors of community for dispersed people. Memory allows for the imaginative construction of the world in which one finds themselves, as well as the one left behind. The memory of place lets one construct a symbolic homeland the relation to which can be reshaped differently in various settings. Memory acts as a tool to fall back on, allowing for a comfort zone to be created in an unfamiliar setting, yet is itself shaped and reconstructed by the very act of migration itself(Burns, 1989). Further paradoxes arise as one's relation with their homeland becomes trapped between a reality of resentment for the very situation which prompted migration in the first place, and the embellishment of everyday actions which have transferred from a category of unmarkedness in the homeland, to one of markedness abroad(Mandel, 1989). For those originating in the post-colonial world, the notion of an imagined space, an imagined homeland is not necessarily a new concept as the concept of an imagined homeland, an imagined place, served as empowering concepts in anti-colonial discourse.

2.3 Nostalgia without memory, the homeland as a repertoire of cultural scenarios residing in the imagination. The alienation and psychological distance afforded by deterritorialization.

The rootless alienation and psychological distance associated with the deterritorialized nation state, the fantasies and nightmares associated with the processes of reterritorialization allow for a unique phenomenon to develop, the concept of nostalgia without memory. A concept which rests on the premise that globalization and the experiences it affords are composed of the image, the imagined, and the imaginary(Appadurai, 1990). Within this context, the past, the homeland, is not viewed as something which can be physically returned to, but rather becomes a repertoire of cultural scenarios to be accessed in accordance with the specific situation at hand(Appadurai, 1990). The culture of everyday practices draws on the notion of a shared history and traditions inasmuch that people can think of themselves as members of a society to the extent that they can occupy a place in that society's history and can identify with the way in which it remembers the past, views the present, and perceives the future(Kramsch, 2000). Imagination leaves the realm of fantasy to become a social practice, a form of negotiation between sites of agency and globally defined fields of possibility mediated through language which, over time, becomes a metaphor for cultural reality.

2.4 Place and space as parts of the global system of domination. Class as the link between social spaces and the material world. Globalizing factors and displacement, culture as travel.

The notion of place, of space within this context consequently becomes part of a global system of domination. At this point, rethinking the intrinsic relations between culture, power, economic spaces(i.e. poverty), allows for combating what Appadurai has referred to as a very literal "spatial incarceration of the native" by changing our very texts in approaching such issues. As space is deterritorialized, it is at the same time reterritorialized from physical space into social space, in that the distance between the privileged of the world is much less than the distance between the privileged and the disenfranchised within a specific locale(Gupta, 1992). Within the construct of globalizing tendencies, social, class differentiation becomes greater than cultural differentiation. With class in itself representing a category defined by the level of alienation from control over means of production, while class for itself represents a group in which the constituents identify with one another in their collective misfortune and have the potential for collective action based on that identification(Jenkins, 2003). The representational challenge which arises when studying culture is the portrayal and understanding of local and global historical encounters. An approach which takes into consideration the processes of domination, resistance, and co-production which define social relations(Clifford, 1992). With social relations being most widely represented by class, as it serves as the main locator of social position, providing the code through which we read one another, understand each other's discourse, and links us to the economy and thus to material life(Hall, 1991).

The view of culture as travel becomes relevant within this context in that traditional approaches to fieldwork have focused on issues of locality rather than the inter-connectedness of cultures, and the questions of uprooted cultures of the post-colonial era. Ethnography has greatly privileged the relations of dwelling over those of travel. By viewing culture as travel, we can look at the negotiation of external relations, whether or not the culture itself is a mode of travel, and at the relationship between the core and the periphery. It also stresses the various modalities of inside-outside connection, that displacement can involve forces which pass through television, radio, tourists, commodities, and armies and is not necessarily intrinsically linked to the notion of the diasporic experience alone. By asserting that class, gender, and race influence travel and location, an approach which allows and favors hyperglossia is enacted(Clifford, 1992). The political and economic factors of displacement cannot be ignored, nor can the role of the Euro-centric, male, bourgeois history associated with the term travel itself. Thus identity becomes an element resting on history, ideology, and social and political structures while the concept of ethnicity is rendered to be a historical topographic accident of birth(Mandel, 1989).

2.4.1 Globalization and the subsequent conflict which it produces. The relationship between the various scapes which define the world and the subjectivity of the imagined. The legacy of colonial and post-colonial struggles, the notion of history, culture, and power being continuously at play with each other.

The global cultural flow can be described as the tension between cultural homogenization and cultural heterogenization. This tension is brought about by the relationship between ethnoscapes, mediascapes, technoscapes, finanscapes, and ideoscapes, which suggest that global cultural systems are driven by the relationship flows of persons, technologies, finance, information, and ideology(Appadurai, 1990). These are deeply perspectival constructs inflected by the historical, linguistic, and political situations of different actors. These scapes are the building blocks of one's perceptions of the world, they create a mythical imagery rather than one approaching objectivity. They are the building blocks of imagined worlds, multiple worlds which are constituted by the historically situated imaginations of persons and groups spread around the globe(Appadurai, 1990). Such an approach takes into mind the problematics of simple visions of ethnicity and nation states as being fixed or immobile. Boundaries tend to be taken for granted while they are stable, becoming problematic only when conflict occurs(Jenkins, 2003).

Such conceptions of culture and identity are the product of colonialism and the consequent post-colonial struggles which have profoundly reshaped, and continue to shape our world. Far from being eternally fixed in an essentialist past, we are all subject to the continuous play of history, culture, and power. A situation in which the world's societies are constructed as "different" and as "other" within the categories of knowledge of the Western world(Hall, 1990). It is within such a context that identity is always in a certain sense a structured representation which only achieves its positive through the narrow eye of the negative(Hall, 1991). While we are in an ever constant state of becoming, we do so under conditions which are not of our own choosing, we become subject to an order based on the premises of globalization. I use the term "order" rather than the more popular term "new world order" simply because as we are beginning to comprehend and think of an idea, this does not necessarily mean that the processes we are thinking about have just begun, on the contrary, like most processes, globalization precedes our comprehension of it. History is filled with examples of nation states, entities of power which are exceedingly dangerous as they ascend since they do so by subjugating others through the use of force and coercion, and as they decline since when they do so they tend to take everyone down with them(Hall, 1991).

2.4.2 The West as the center of globalizing movements, the enigma of the capitalist world view. Position as definitive of truth and meaning.

Throughout history, globalizing movements expressed via colonialism, imperialism, globalization, neo-liberalism, have remained centered in the West. Conceptions of Western technology, the concentration of capital in the West, Western techniques, the concentration of advanced labor in Western societies, the stories and imagery of the West, have all maintained themselves as the driving force of global mass culture(Hall, 1991). Consequently, capitalist thought tends to be absolutist in the attribution of positive qualities to capitalist intentions, actions, and achievements and in the imputation of evil motives and pernicious actions to the representatives of the non-capitalist, non-Western world. Capitalist behavior and thought have proven to be difficult to understand and deal with because they are based on the denial of alternate patterns to exist. Exceptional intolerance has usually been displayed towards domestic ideological and cultural pluralism as well as towards non-Western, non-capitalist movements of self determination, and those groups believing in the concept of modernization without Westernization, in the world. The capitalist, or Western world view is based on a dialectical division of the world into capitalist," free," pro-Western, and "hostile," "undemocratic" nation states and political, cultural movements. Westernized, capitalist nations thus represent the only possible incarnation of "legitimate" regimes and forms of expression within this world view(Said, 1993). The capitalist world view becomes more perplex as the discourse of value cannot be escaped. The conjuncture of the notions of "Western" and "non-Western" creates a text within which are organized the aesthetics of every day life. Within this text, choices are made which have value, yet the value of such choices is not made according to any intrinsic worth, but rather on the possible thought's or object's position in the system of both social and material production and exchange(Lancaster, 2003). Such an order of perceived value makes sense only in terms that it is validated(Frow, 1998), that it is upheld by the beliefs of a community of meanings. It constitutes a broad set of arguments concerning what is desirable, reasonable, who can demand what and in which circumstances(Frow, 1998). As such judgments of value are mere choices made within a particular regime, problems of positionality arise, namely the paradoxes surrounding what gets more value, why, who speaks for whom, who is listened to, who is not, what is right, wrong, who can speak for others, and why and how does such discourse shift(Frow, 1998).

The author of discourse is not the source of the utterance itself, but rather merely the one accredited with it, as positional location determines truth and meaning. This approach to the world is dominated by an unprecedented expectation of conflict. In state societies, public and private domains are constructed and penetrated by the institutions and interests of the state. It must then be kept in mind that in the age of globalization, the personal is linked to the political, the domestic to the public, as identity is created through the various negotiations and pathways which bind an individual to a specific nation, or in the case of transmigrants to two or more nations(Fouron, 2001).

2.5 Defining the term transmigrant. The concept of transnationalist as a direct product of Westernization. Rawl's "Theory of Justice." Discrimination techniques of governments as directly linked to techniques of social validation. Ethnic identity as a tool in the hands of the elite.

Transmigrants differ from other forms of migrants in that they live within transnational social fields, what can be defined as "an unbounded terrain of interlocking egocentric networks that extends across borders of two or more nation-states and that incorporates its participants in the day-to-day activities of social reproduction in these various locations"(Fouron, 2001). Thus these individuals' actions take place within the constraints of power structures which lie within the territory and legal systems of more than one state, with each limiting, disciplining, and shaping their identity(Fouron, 2001).

Transnationalism itself is a product of the apparent conflict produced by globalizing trends while at the same time contributing to the conflict itself, leaving us with much to learn about the interconnection between the two factors. The notion of "development," or better said "Westernization," promises an end to social problems and economic misery yet only creates new dimensions and definitions of human bondage(Gonzalez, 1989). As the benefits of the so-called "development" produced by global economic currents becomes unequally distributed, migration becomes a force of leverage by the disenfranchised as they seek to appropriate what they view as their fair share of the West's wealth by physically transferring themselves to the West itself(Gonzalez, 1989). Transnationalism arises from the failure of modern states to meet the needs of their citizens, to resolve and manage disputes, and better control economic and territorial competition. The age of modernity can in itself be said to be the age of capitalist failure, as it has created a system of privilege and great benefit for a few, while leaving the great majority in a state of oppression, the lack of rights, and with no sense of respect for their value systems(Gonzalez, 1989). The notion of social justice in capitalism is based on the "Theory of Justice," by John Rawls, which simply states that those who are off badly are well off enough to survive and that they simply complain about their state of being out of envy for those who have accomplished more(Eagleton, 1998). Such political failure acts to promote conflict on all levels of society, as all are intertwined with ideology. When contact is made between transmigrants and their host society, it is the contact between two voices, accents, languages, forms of consciousness, a collision between two world views, with negotiation occurring in the territory of utterances, of discourse(Bhabha, 1998). Yet it represents not only the potential for conflict, but also the potential for compromise, as it creates a situation pregnant with the potential for new world views, for perceiving the world in new words.

For the most part, transnationals have been met with xenophobia and social aggression as techniques of government are tied closely to techniques of social validation(Chakrabarty, 1998). In the United States of America, a conservative reaction based on antiquarian iconography has formed to the politics of representation, thus avoiding and in effect disallowing multicultural practice on an aesthetic level(Koundoura, 1998). In such a context, begetting the "right kind of national pride" remains the goal as ethnic identity becomes a tool in the hands of the elite who determine the prestige culture and its boundaries(Mathieson, 1998). The concept of nation becomes a political move which denies history, while the political sphere becomes inept at negotiating social conflict. Both civil society and the state move into an illusionary realm of perceived general will and rational freedom where symbolic practice enters the public sphere(Koundoura, 1998). Signifiers are then found to fill empty signifieds and imbue them with meaning, a meaning that has been metaleptically constructed in order to hide the politics behind the notion of believing that the institutions and constructs of the nation are "natural." In this manner, nationality rests on political antecedents(Koundoura, 1998).

2.5.1 Nationalism in the United States. The concept of nation and its patterning along the general paradigms of capitalistic logic.

The concept of the nation has symbolic force in so far as it can be prescribed as a single unit, the notion of multiculturalism is by its very nature incompatible with such a view, as it is taken to be an act of subversion of the unified vision of "America"(Stratton, 1998). Rather, official practice concerning transmigrants remains to be assimilation, as American patriotism rests on the legitimacy of the first colonists and their ideological, as well as physical struggles. It depends on the subordination of any "other" identity to that of the United States(Bennett, 1998), the melting of the particular into the universal. The "difference blind" eyes of the state support this notion, turning the concept of equality into a mere social arrangement rather than a complex ontological affair(Eagleton, 1998). The true notion of equality, which entails paying equal attention to the specific needs and desires of particular groups, of focusing on difference and nurturing it, threatens national cohesion as it is thought of in the American world view. Therefore, assimilation, or Americanization is an intentional effort, coercive and prescribed by the guardians of the existing social order(Rumbaut, 2003). Assimilation is ultimately based on a linear logic of positivist narrative which correlates the foreign with inferiority and the domestic with superiority(Rumbaut, 2003).

2.5.2 The will of the "other" and the struggle for multiculturalism. American culture as a based directly on capitalist ideology and its inherent inability to be conducive to multiculturalism.

The struggle for multiculturalism, for the equal recognition of the other, has been initiated by transnationals, as well as other minority groups which feel excluded from national discourse. As an idea, and abstract notion, multiculturalism acts as an affirmation of that exclusion, of the failure of the modern nation state which focuses on unity as sameness at the expense of true equality and diversity(Stratton, 1998). This failure is a product of the Enlightenment originated ideology which views corporate liberalism as the only "natural" expression of the nation state. Consequently, the laissez-faire approach leaves the historically, politically, economically, and socially disenfranchised to fend for themselves, knowing full well that given their circumstances, they can never reach an equal footing with members of the prestige culture(Stratton, 1998). While language is the key to cultural assimilation, fluency is nearly impossible to attain as long as the infrastructure to attain it does not exist(Rumbaut, 2003). Transmigrants live at or near the bottom of the socioeconomic ladder because of the lack of opportunities to get ahead, and more importantly the lack of a social structure which offers structural resources to rely on for the bettering of one's lot in life(Levitt, 2003). Consequently, they watch the Anglo world from the margins, not knowing how to nor being able to negotiate their way in.

In the United States, ideology takes on cultural characteristics, and becomes the very interpretation of what it means to belong to the "American nation." National identity has been formed through ideological means rather than cultural ones, being a settler society, in effect ironically a "multicultural" entity to begin with, there was a need for the invention of a focus point for an "American" identity(Stratton, 1998). Based on the British traditions brought by the first settlers, and which ultimately came to form the substratum of what is today known as American culture, the political theory of John Locke came to be the national ideology(Stratton, 1998). The newly invented American identity came to focus on the assumption of a new nation built on the basis of universal ideological principles which transcend cultural and ethnic specificity. Through the belief in the portability of the "American life," a culture based on ideology was created(Stratton, 1998). Mainstream society, as well as sociology support this view of American culture based on the sharing of norms, values, and attitudes(Stratton, 1998). American prestige culture, as based on the norms and values of the white, heterosexual, middle class views itself is threatened by contamination from cultural, linguistic, racial, and sexual differences(Giroux, 1998). Such a view leads to ideals of homogenization and assimilation as those features solidify the universality of values. Within such a context, minorities are seen as a threat for not sharing those values perceived as "universal." Thus, otherness is constructed as being negative, as a potential danger, the residue of the melting process, or those who have "failed" to become "real Americans"(Stratton, 1998). In reality, the assimilation to America's prestige culture fails because the American ideal of a "promised land" fails to materialize, leading to a state of disillusion with the United States(Stratton, 1998). Such a failure is not a shortcoming of the system, but is rather structurally constitutive of the social formation of the nation. It represents the ideological failure of the myth of opportunity for all, the myth of liberty, human rights, of creating and exporting democracy, progress, and prosperity (Stratton, 1998). American nationalism creates a discourse which neatly links nation, culture, and citizenship, while the past is negotiated and renegotiated through the politics of remembering and forgetting. Thus providing a defense for the narratives of the dominant culture, legitimating an exceedingly narrow and bigoted image of what it means to be American(Giroux, 1998). The national discourse and narrative of the United States is based on ethnocentric pretensions as it conflates the real with the rhetorical, idea with ideal and ideological, descriptions with prescriptions, in an attempt to support national illusions(Rumbaut, 2003). Such an approach views any critique of society and nation as antithetical to both the construction of national identity and the precepts of patriotism. It is organized around a view of nationalism, of being American that stigmatizes any disagreement by reverting to the "us" vs. "them" dichotomy by automatically labeling critics as anti-American. Such an approach inherently fails to portray the nation as an imagined community that can only be understood within the intersecting dynamics of history, language, ideology, and power(Giroux, 1998).Yet its strength in American society can be exemplified by the backlash against multiculturalism in academia, the rise of the English Only movement, the role of the state as a stern parent willing to inflict harsh measures on welfare mothers, and warmongering, as well as by the portrayal of crime as a nonwhite issue, implying a reductionist correlation between culture and race, by the media's association of the term minority with representations of urban decay, and attacks on immigration and thus immigrants(Giroux, 1998). Capitalist ethics are fed merely by the desire for new sources of profits, a culture will be reached out to, glorified, or made chic in an attempt to economically exploit it. While on the other hand the mass media, the purpose of which is to weaken any opposition to hegemony, censors the public's knowledge of certain cultural expressions(i.e. music, fashion) on purpose(Gruzinski, 2002).

2.5.3 American social reality as the product of a hegemonic universalism based o the policy of exclusion. An introduction to the notion of "Hispanic" and linguicism within the American world view.

The American social reality is the effect of a hegemonic universalism based on the structural centrality of policies of exclusion in the formation of the United States, with the most pronounced exclusionary category being race(Stratton, 1998). The American way of life becomes a pervasive homogenized mass culture of consumerism, with race as a category crucial to political hierarchy and social relationships. With the construct of the color line, race is relegated to otherness, while ethnicity is relegated to white society. It is out of this mind set that the notion of the category of "Hispanic" as being associated with race rather than ethnicity arises(Stratton, 1998). Even though it is in effect a supranational cultural identity that is exclusively linguistic(Kramsch, 2000).

Which brings to mind further issues, within the framework of the American world view, language is viewed as a shared patrimony, a self contained, autonomous, homogeneous linguistic system based on a homogeneous social world(Kramsch, 2000). Language acquires a symbolic value beyond that of pragmatic use and becomes a totem of perceived cultural "sameness" from which arises the deliberate, centralized pressure of a melting pot ideology to impose one language on others. Ultimately, the totemization of the dominant culture leads to the stigmatization of the dominated. In the long run, it becomes expressed as the exercise of the deliberate planning of diffuse societal forces, such as the pressure and coercion used to impose English as "the" international language(Kramsch, 2000). A state of linguicism exists in the United States when it comes to its dealings with the Hispanic community, a condition in which ideology, social structure, and cultural practices are used to legitimate, affectuate, and reproduce the unequal division of power and resources between groups based on the basis of language(Kramsch, 2000). Such linguistic imperialism fails to view linguistic rights as basic human rights.

2.5.4 Reactions to linguicism. The language of the oppressed as taking on a new markedness as a symbol of resistance. Citizenship as not being definitive of belonging to American society and the consequent viewing of the host society as the locus of conflict. The effects of such processes on identity.

However, when a group feels that its cultural and political identity is threatened, the group's language gains particular importance as a source of identity and legitimation. Language becomes a tool which signifies solidarity with one's own group, while also expressing distance from the "other." It signifies who one accepts as a member of their community, and who accepts them, thus becoming a strategy of resistance, of reaffirming their identity and notion of difference within the sphere of homogenizing forces, becoming a cultural act of identity(Kramsch, 2000).

It is because of such social constructs that living in the United States, speaking the language, participating in the economy, does not make one an American. The essence of the concept of nation is a psychological bond that joins and differentiates, it is not based on what is, but on what people perceive it to be(Walker, 2003). Factual history is not the foundation of the nation but rather sentient history, what is felt. Such feelings, sets of beliefs are impacted by population movements, globalizing trends, which split national identity between the past and the present, the self and the other(Walker,

2003). The impact of the other threatens the national homogenous narrative as it has the potential to reveal the fragmented character of identity, an unsettling idea for those who spend their existence within the confines of the narrative of hegemony, no matter how involuntary or unconscious that confinement might be(Walker, 2003). Notions of self and other present themselves as plastic, malleable social constructions derived from the power relations between individuals and groups who invoke them. The concepts exist only as the discourse of fictive identity within the hegemonic constraints of society(Walker, 2003).

2.6 Historical antecedence of alienation, isolation, conflicting world views, and the imagined homeland among Hispanics.

Yet the host society is not the only source of conflict in shaping the identity and world views of transnationals, as they bring with them the paradoxes of nation building inherent to their homelands. The world view of Hispanic transmigrants is the product of 500 years of colonialism, resistance, and processes of creolization. Latin America can rightfully be said to be the product of the first globalizing factors, the first world economy, as during the early colonial phase from 1570 to 1640 Spain and Portugal economically dominated Western Europe, while they politically dominated the Americas, the coasts of Africa, and had asserted their ambitions in the Philippines, Nagasaki, Macao, Cochin, Goa, and the Chinese coast(Gruzinski, 2002).

This initial contact of worlds, known as globalization, or Westernization, had as strong an impact on society then as it does now. Communication between the two worlds was marked by confusion, it was not contact between two cultures but between fragments of multiple worlds which did not remain in contact for long. The constraints, vagueness, and conflict mirrored those encountered by cultural contacts today(Gruzinksi, 2002). Opposing elements of cultures in contact tend to be mutually exclusive and confronting, while at the same time they tend to interpenetrate, combining and identifying with each other, giving birth to a new world view born out of the interpenetration and combination of opposites. Perhaps the foundations of what we today perceive as Latin American culture can best be described in the words of Motolinia, a Spanish monk present at the fall of Mexico City to the Spaniards in 1521, in his life work he recalls, "When we saw the land through our inner vision, it appeared filled with great shadows, thrust into the mayhem of transgression and total disorder"(Gruzinski, 2002). Yet the spaces in between produced by colonialism provided the location and energy of new modes of thinking whose strength lies in the transformation and critique of the authenticities of both the Western and the Amerindian legacies. Such borders are porous, permeable, flexible, mobile, as they provide the sudden passage from one world to another(Gruzinski, 2002). The meaning of culture itself becomes something to be weary of however, as it stamps reality with an obsession for order, analysis, and formulation that is specific to modernity. It conveys authenticity to the core and inauthenticity to the periphery, creating notions of pure and contaminated. It becomes an amorphous cluster in perpetual motion rather than a well defined system(Gruzinski, 2002).

2.7 Aspects of social conflict imported by Hispanics from Latin America, classism, racism, colorism, and Hispanidad.

Hispanics bring with them to the United States a notion of identity, race, and ethnicity intrinsically linked to a system where the value of a person is determined within a system of exchanges in terms of relations between lexical clusters around color, an institution which began with the Spanish conquest and stipulates the superiority of Spanish culture and phenotype(Lancaster, 2003). The politics of the Spanish conquest have not been lost in discourse, creating a society at war with itself, one where Spanish culture battles Amerindian skin. Such discourse is very subtle and individual, resting on ways of perceiving the self in contrast to others, and on the political implications of everyday discourse deemed apolitical(Lancaster, 2003). What can be viewed as colorism rather than racism rests on a series of mostly contingent and contextual discursive gestures. Yet it exists as a practice rather than as a structure as no race boundary exists where discourse and negotiation cease, it rather consists of concentric circles as power plays(Lancaster, 2003). Colorism rests on a complex phenotypic system based on features, hair structure, and a range of skin tones. It is not an ideology per se, but rather the engagement of self with other in society and history, based on one's political and economic position within the context of the reproduction of the history of repression through race relations(Lancaster, 2003). It represents the struggle for a voice within a system of privilege and power based on one's location within a system of contrasts. A system of contrasts in which whiteness and darkness exist in a dialectic opposition to each other, as individuals negotiate their way through the grey area in between the two poles. With whiteness representing the prestige culture, whiteness, Spanishness, the legacy of the "victors" of the conquest. While darkness is related to poverty, backwardness, and subjugation(Lancaster, 2003). However, color and race alone do not determine one's category within the system as one's language, place of birth, and way of dress come into play as well, with that most approximating Spanish norms and values being the most highly valued. The system is a way in which the Spanish conquest is relived symbolically as well as materially by every generation. Such an approach is inherently based on self deprecation for the masses as someone is always in a constant quest to portray themselves as lighter than someone else, while viewing themselves as darker than others, it becomes a construct of maximizing oneself at the expense of minimizing others(Lancaster, 2003). At the same time, moments of reprieve and flashes of rebellion abound as with the example of the carnival celebrations in Latin America where the "other" is elevated over "whiteness." As well as in the appropriation of negative categories and turning them into positive ones, such as the use of negro/a(black) as a term of affection rather than one of invectiveness as is commonly done(Lancaster, 2003). While social classes are based on the movement of racial categories with ambiguous margins, the Amerindian heritage becomes appreciated only so long as it remains frozen in history or art, as to associate today's oppressed Amerindian population with the pre-Columbian civilizations is threatening as it questions and contests the legitimacy of the Spanish elite(Bueno, 1998). The power of discourse, or the discourse of power, feeds on the despair of defeat more than on the energy of domination. The colonial hegemony of the Spanish conquest maintains its presence through the exercise of power through innumerable, nonegalitarian and mobile relations of interplay. It acts as a strategic, intentional, non-subjective system which already accounts for resistances and divisionary tactics by targets, which by no means threaten power, a power which is ultimately not owned nor held, but firmly implanted in both body and discourse(Lancaster, 2003).

2.8 The clash of Hispanic and American world views, differences in ways of classifying the "other."

As processes of ethnic, or racial awareness are intertwined with experiences and expectations of racial and ethnic discrimination, conflict occurs as in the United States, a solid structure of race is encountered where Hispanic is deemed to be "brown," and no official sliding discourse of color exists(Lancaster, 2003). While whiteness in the Unites States represents a state of hegemonic dominance, it does not act as a category nor as an identity but is rather associated with the norm, white is equal to "normal," relegating all else to the category of "other"(Roy, 2003). Within such a new and unfamiliar context, things previously taken for granted are appropriated to higher positions by transmigrants. The conscious construction of identity becomes interactive, in that one's actions and perceptions correlate directly to the reactions which they receive(Langer, 1998). Within this context, a state of internal talk develops, careful choices are made about what is said to whom, define community and indicate choices of political action. To talk internally selects listeners and shows people where they locate themselves in society, defines the inner and the outer worlds, distinguishes between ally and enemy, peer and oppressor, while to make such talk public constitutes an attempt to change one's world(Roy, 2003). Differences between private and public talk maps power relationships, secrecy and subterfuge are acts of resistance or rebellion by people lacking more overt sources for pursuing political objectives. While the ability to complain in safe quarters makes tolerating intolerable situations somewhat more tolerable(Roy, 2003). People in vulnerable positions pay attention to nuances which affect their opportunity for advancement, chances for expression, and in which the ability to prevail in conflicts is reflected. It creates solidarity among sufferers, defines groups capable of taking action when appropriate, and keeps alive the spirit of dignified resistance to oppression, while defining the local world in contrast to the outside(Roy, 2003). Cultural forms and traditions become destabilized by centrifugal currents from the metropolis and mass media, which in turn causes new cultural forms to arise that resist, neutralize, or corrupt the terror and abjection associated with the struggle to represent the oppressed, to give a voice to marginality(Bueno, 1998). Thus enabling the ability to embody the discursive resources by which people articulate the meanings of their subordination. Yet even if subverted, hegemony cannot be escaped as all cultural production depends on a legitimation of sorts by hegemonic ideology(Bueno, 1998).

2.9 The role of language among transnationals. Its role as a mobilizing structure among Hispanics.

With language being the basis of community as well as class among transnationals, the notion of a "Spanish speaking community" rests on the impossible separation of language and culture from class, politics, and history. Yet it also serves as an alternate way of recognizing competing claims of national groups whose boundaries and claims are continuously contested and renegotiated. The fiction of community remains as a hegemonic achievement of those who mobilized it as a rhetorical strategy in competition for the distribution of state resources(Langer, 2003). While at the same time acting as an alternative to nostalgia as a mobilizing structure, as the practices of oppressed groups and classes contain within them the resources for imagining an alternative for a future society(Bueno, 1998). Such a world view becomes a subcultural response of the marginalized to the specific historical circumstances which they encounter.

2.10   Historical antecedents of contact between the United States and Latin America, the case of Mexico. The previously described processes at work.

Conflict and marginalization have marked the relation between the dominant culture of the United States and Hispanic societies since the earliest days of contact. With the case of Mexico, Mexicans were viewed as being impure both racially and morally by the population and regime of the United States since the very conception of that nation, due mainly to the fact that Mexico was born a Catholic nation, with Spanish culture, and a population which was mostly the product of miscegenation between Spaniards and the indigenous Amerindian population(Bueno, 1998). It was this negative image and discourse which was used to justify the conquest of 1859, as Mexico became the other against which white American society constructed itself as being superior to. The commonly perceived image of Mexicans as being degenerate, lazy, stupid, and inherently criminal has changed little in American history(Bueno, 1998). Unfortunately, such notions even became internalized among Mexicans living in the United States. As little ago as 1942, an organization called the Mexican American Movement was formed on the basis of calling for white help to help rid the Mexican population of California of its "inherent backwardness" through more aggressive assimilation campaigns(Bueno, 1998).

2.10.1 The Pachuco movement, a historical antecedent to the present day situation of Hispanics in the United States, and as a reaction of resistance to hegemony.

As a response to such negative attitudes, and actions, open resistance arose through the guise of the Pachuco movement, which constituted a proud assertion of difference which was troubling for hegemony, a sign that the social order had failed to contain their energy and their difference(Bueno, 1998). The Pachuco became the aesthetic product of migration, an icon whose gestures, clothes, whose very way of being was seen as a provocation in white eyes, and thus the Pachuco was thrown into the position of an involuntary symbol of cultural resistance, and consequently of persecution(Bueno, 1998). Yet the issue was more complex, the distinct mannerisms, and way of dress, including the infamous zoot suit, pinned the Pachuco between two worlds, seen as too Mexican by Americans, and as too American by Mexicans, a new identity was being negotiated along the margins of two ethnocentric ideals.

As the Pachuco straddled the borders of two worlds, a militant ethnic and cultural pride developed as the subculture's hallmarks. The world of the Pachuco was a dangerous one, as the United States was engaged in the Second World War, a homogenous identity was being propagated at home in order to foster a stronger sense of patriotism and support for the war, anything or anyone different became automatically associated with deviance(Bueno, 1998). The perceived threat of the Pachuco to American "homogeneity" was such that in 1942 it became illegal to manufacture zoot suits, as a 26% cut back on the use of fabrics was enacted. The zoot suit was seen as a threat not only because of its association with the Pachuco and the "Harlem Dude," but also because of its cut, which to many represented a parody of the bourgeois suit, and consequently a rejection of bourgeois values(Bueno, 1998). The situation was such, that in 1943 the Zoot Suit Riots broke out in Los Angeles. On May 1, 1943, coal miners in Pennsylvania went on strike, the act provoked high tension on the east coast as physical conflict between military servicemen and citizens deemed to be "unpatriotic" escalated, leaving seven dead in that month alone. By June, the tensions had spread to the west coast as off duty service men and "patriotic" civilians entered Mexican barrios in Los Angeles, stripped the Pachucos, and cut their hair(Bueno, 1998). Surprisingly no one was killed in the Zoot Suit Riots, as the purpose seemed to be not to kill the Pachucos, but to perform a symbolic castration of their identity, of asserting the power of hegemony and its unwillingness to accept the other as is, to assert the ideology of ideological sameness behind American nationalism and identity. The image of the Pachuco, of pachuquismo as a reaction to white racism, the embodiment of open resistance to cultural emasculation, remains(Bueno, 1998). Such a history sets the arena for any discourse on Hispanic identity in the United States today.

2.11   Language as relevant to the discourse of identity. Its role as the locus of meaning.

Any such discourse cannot ignore the role of language in the formation of identity and the negotiation between two worlds. Language allows for the creation and reformulation of competing vehicles of symbolic thought which make up culture to the new power structures which culture contact creates. Within this context, language takes on the meaning of a complex semiotic system relying not merely on verbal communication but also on the most diverse forms of media, the plastic arts, dance, music, and poetry. Language not only expresses cultural reality, but also embodies and symbolizes it by being the medium through which experience is created as well as expressed.

As language is the most sensitive indicator of the relationship between an individual and society, it indexes our relationship to the world as it allows us to express alternately played out social identities within the complex framework of daily encounters, becoming an arena in which our cultural allegiances and loyalties are fought out as the crossing of borders, whether literal or symbolic, causes conflict(Kramsch, 2000).

2.12 Relevance of the literary sources chosen.

The literary sources involved in the writing and inspiration of this work were selected on their merit in aiding the understanding of the conditions which are responsible for the creation of transnationalism, as well as in enhancing the understanding of identity formation among transnationals. With the Hispanic populace of the United States being the largest transnational community in the world, I deemed the works relevant to the situation encountered by that population as well as any other transnational group.

2.12.1 The dislocation of space and reterritorialization.

Gupta's focus on the challenge of the creation of space within the spheres of memory and imagination, Edward Said's notion of a generalized condition of homelessness, Burns' theory of identity as being shaped and reshaped by the physical and psychological act of migration, and Appadurai's concept of the imagined homeland serve as basic tenets when approaching any discussion of identity among migrant populations.

2.12.2 Studies of transnationals focusing on globalization fail to address historical antecedents. Studies of class, race, and ethnicity within the context of globalization as focusing on the mechanics rather than the human aspects of the transnational experience.

These basic tenets have been built upon by scholars who have taken a closer look at aspects of the transnational experience, notably Clifford and Hall who have focused on globalization, namely class and social prestige as cultural markers linking a group to an economic system and consequently to means of production and distribution of material goods. Along the same lines, Gonzalez treats transnationalism as arising from the failure of modern states to meet the needs of their citizens, resolve and manage disputes, and adequately control economic and territorial competition. However, while addressing their specific points of focus in an adequate manner, none of these scholars addresses the connection between present day situations and historical antecedents in the relationships between groups where an asymmetrical power relationship in constant flux exists.

Glick Schiller and Blanc-Szanton(1992) take things a bit further by describing the interconnectedness of migration, race, class, ethnicity, and nationalism in the shaping and reshaping of identity. While accomplishing what they set out to do, they do it in a manner which looks at those issues too mechanically. The focus lies exclusively on material aspects such as the influence of global economic flows, remittances, the advertising media, and the affects of a clash between two or more materially different cultures on identity. The subtle nuances associated with contact, the emotional implications, the feelings which people have and why they have them, as well as the clash and neutralization of world views and their constant negotiations and renegotiations are not addressed.

2.12.3 A review of Fouron's work. His focus on discourse, but consequent neglect of the role of language itself.

Georges Fouron(2001), the scholar whose work on Haitian Americans, has been highly influential as an inspiration and somewhat of a model for my work, took the stakes a notch higher. Fouron was influenced by Homi Bhabha's notion of contact between two cultures as being in effect the contact between two voices, accents, languages, world views, that discourse is in effect the territory of negotiation in culture contact. Consequently, the issue of the power of discourse, discourse as power, gender, and the penetrations of state institutions into the private domain from their public abodes figures greatly in his writings. Identity becomes viewed as having been created through the various negotiations and pathways which bind the individual to the nation. Day to day activities are focused on as all of an individual's actions take place with the constraints of power structures. However, he places a focus on the grand narrative of Haiti and its affect upon the various perceptions of "being Haitian" among the Haitians of Miami, with the bulk of his work focusing on the dichotomy between the French and African models of thought in the Haitian mind.

2.12.4 Literary sources as having been chosen in order to aid in understanding the role of pan-identities and historical antecedence in identity formation. As well as an aid to address previously ignored issues.

While focusing on the achievements of Fouron et al, I then selected literary sources which aid in uncovering issues which those scholars did not address. My goal was to create a theoretical framework with which to view transnational identity on a different level, one which focuses on the historical antecedents of current situations, which does not ignore nor skim over the role of language as an identity marker, and which allows for a discussion of the role of pan-identities in determining their role in power negotiations and discourse.

The great majority of the literature I have come into contact with fails to address the role of language within transnational processes with adequate emphasis. Likewise, despite covering mostly Caribbean and Latin American transnational communities, no one has placed a significant focus on the role of pan-identities such as "West Indian" or "Hispanic." When the notion of a Hispanic pan-identity is dealt with, it is more often than not done so within the framework of "constructing minorities" rather than transnationalism, or as a concept which parallels the Bolivarian narrative and ideal of Latin Americanism which stipulates a single continental entity united by the Spanish language and the anti-colonial, anti-imperial struggle. The concept of the Spanish language as an identity marker among transnational groups tends to be viewed the same way. In turn, what I have sought to do is to address a common issue in a manner which places an emphasis on uncommonly addressed elements of the transnational experience.

2.12.5 The development of a workable theoretical model. The connection between data and theory.

The end goal of selecting the various literary sources was to help me create a theoretical model which could be applied to the study of any situation where a history of ongoing migration and asymmetrical power relationships in constant flux between two or more groups, nation states, or other entities is present. While allowing for a focus on the commonly ignored features of language, pan-identity, and historical antecedence within this specific context.

While my work's fieldwork in the city of Las Vegas is the first of its kind, the theoretical contributions gained through literary research are of importance as well. Fieldwork gains life when it is placed into a framework, a story, which makes sense of it by knitting together the wide range of various odds and ends observed. However, to point to the discursive production of reality does not deny its materiality. What it does is point to the crucial role of discourse as the locus of meaning.

CHAPTER 3
Setting the Context

3.0 A deconstruction of the concept of "labels."

Labels of any sort are the product of hegemony, they are never free of ideology as when they are applied, the author knows not only the literal or scholarly intent of that label, but also the implications which that label holds within the context of mainstream culture. A lack of clarity and deconstruction of the very label itself, symbolizes the author's own ideological agenda of supporting the status quo of society through means of the notion of propter nos, or the notion that one's own way is the "right" way as legitimized by the precepts of assigning a prestige position to one's own world view and supporting that position through an intricate series of paradigms which define and legitimize one's own logic. Labels which are intended to identify a "minority group," in effect a population which the majority considers inferior as it has been historically oppressed for generations and is socially rejected, economically excluded, and lacks political power. The language of race and ethnicity is mired in euphemisms which serve to support stereotypes, misconceptions, and half truths. For example, the term "poor" is often euphemized as "disadvantaged" while it is often used as a synonym for a person who does not ascribe to the dominant culture's definition of "whiteness." Various terms such as the sociological term "urban," or the geographical term "inner city," and even the economical term "blue collar" connote race and ethnicity. The label Hispanic or Latin are euphemisms for referring to important sectors of the United States working class. Within the context of American capitalism, it is legitimate to state political claims only as members of ethnic or racial minorities or majorities but not in terms of class locations. The lack of challenges to this situation allows for the perpetuation of perceptions which strengthen the racial and ethnic divisions among people and thus racism itself. The status quo allows for individuals to have a voice in the expression of their grievances so long as they portray themselves as the victims of their race, gender, or ethnicity, but not as victims of the capitalist system.

In reality, when dealing with labels, it is necessary to realize that to label others is a reflection of one's own affiliation to that label. A part of others' categorization is in fact a mirror image, a reflection, of one's own fundamental beliefs, for which they must answer as well. There are several questions which need to be answered when one deals with any label. Who is labeling whom? Why do they label them? How is the one labeling seen by those whom they label? What moral authority does one have to ascribe labels to others based on one's own perceived ethical and cultural standards?

3.1 A deconstruction of the notion of "discourse."

Discourse is an artificially restrictive paradigm of knowledge creation. It excludes those ideas which fall outside of its boundaries. That exclusion, the ability to shape thought and ultimately truth, is the factory of power masked by the very nature of discourse. A system of control by which the very nature of reality is dictated, mediated, and ultimately self-reified. Discourse does not represent truth but rather creates it. The concept of labeling the "other" is such that it can only exist in a dialectical relationship, as such notions arise with the concept of the perception of having the "absolute truth," which serves as the paradigm for labeling the "other" on the basis of "inauthenticity" in contrast to oneself for having a competing "absolute truth" which defines their sense of being, of belonging to a specific group, In this way, one is able to categorize and label someone as being "other," as inauthentic in contrast to one's own "authentic" group identity.

Discourse shapes history, and history seeks to fit singular events into larger theories. Meanings of those events change as the popular opinions change and new events that are added are only added insofar as they support the existing historical paradigm. Within this context all new historical understanding must fit into the boundaries of discourse, thus the reality of yesteryear is shaped by the discourse of today. As every work is marked by the ideological and class position of its author, the authors of officialdom present under a cover of the "quest for truth" the defense of capitalist interests and values and the ideological preconceptions of the Western, industrialized, capitalist world. They have accepted an idealist view of history based on the powers of imagination and fantasy in which a few individuals have the power to destroy or create progress rather than viewing history as a complex system of negotiation between the powers and constraints within a given society, and between various societies. Historical processes allow for the creation and reformulation of competing vehicles of symbolic thought which make up culture. To adopt another view of our world, of its institutions, paradigms, means looking at ourselves, our history, and our world through the eyes of the oppressed and exploited classes of capitalism.

3.2 Language transformations as integral aspects associated with culture change and culture contact.

Language transformations define culture in that they are the ways in which sense is made of the surrounding world. Changes in language allow for the transformation of a finite set of underlying structures into infinitely varied yet culturally marked expressions, culture is not a meaning loaded underlying structure nor an infinite corpus of expressions, it is rather the process of negotiation between them. It allows for culture to be a way for individuals to situate themselves in the human landscape, a way of making sense, it is not separate from the people constructing it. While culture change is not analogous to language change, it is a related system of representation that both affects and is affected by language.

3.3 Th discourse of transnationalism as the discourse of globalization. The link between race, capitalism, colonialism and power in historical antecedents to the present day situation. A treatment of the United States within a post-colonial context.

Consequently, the discourse of transnationalism, which is invariably the discourse of globalizing processes, is deeply rooted in the culture change associated with the various phases of capitalistic evolution. It begins with colonialism, which represents the capitalistic phase of primitive accumulation by centralizing European states. It used coerced forms of labor which in turn created racial and/or ethnic differences in the workforce. It culminated in the creation of the conditions necessary for the emergence of full industrial capitalism in Europe, and its associated political forms such as nationalist class societies, as well as laid down the foundations for what is today the continually exploited third world. Within the colonial context, slavery and de-facto slavery enter the picture, the social status where a person and their labor power are owned as a thing by one who has complete rights to dispose of them as a capital asset, the notion of segregation by race also appears. Race is more than the physical or somatic traits used to establish differences between people. It is a pathological consequence of capitalist development of which the social aspect is the most important. Race does not exist in people themselves but in their interpersonal relationships, and the value placed on those relationships within the context of the hierarchy of power. The concept of race consequently became a badge of status within the origins hierarchy in the antinomy between freedom and servitude. An ideological dualism existed in the colonial world: native/white, slave/free. Indigenous, or better said, peoples of non-European origins, formed a culture of dispossession given an aura of legitimacy by doctrines of discovery and conquest, treaties, and the "gift of civilization." The non-European peoples in a colony are not allowed a valid interpretation of their culture and history because the conquered do not write their own history. They must endure a history which shames them, destroys their confidence, and causes them to reject their own culture. Imperialism systematically denies oppressed peoples their dignity. In order to "reform" the conquered mind, colonialism assigns positive traits to Western civilization while through perverted logic negating the validity of the "other." The United States is curiously often excluded from postcolonial studies of culture and imperialism in that it is either absorbed into a generalized notion of the "West" along with Europe, or is taken to stand for a monolithic "West." Either scenario treats the continental expansion of the United States as an entirely separate phenomenon from the European colonialism of the nineteenth century, instead of as an interrelated form of imperial expansion. The historians of the United States often suffer from a self imposed historical amnesia which sugar coats the nation's behavior with the notion of "exceptions."

3.3.1 The capitalistic stage of primitive accumulation. The so-called "Third World" as a direct product of colonialism. Globalization as a continuation of colonial processes. Capitalism as responsible for the phenomenon of transnationalism and the conditions which cause it to occur.

The quest for raw materials and labor to create industrialization in the West came at the cost of the rape of 3 continents, Asia, Africa, and the Americas. According to the United Nations, it cost the lives of 100 million Native Americans, 80 million Indians, and 210 million Africans to set up the economic base upon which industrialization could be possible. When full industrialization did occur, it was applied at the cost of severe environmental damage, child labor, wage slavery, and 14 hour work days. Today, it has culminated in 385 persons being wealthier than two billion, three hundred thousand others(Bonilla, 1985). Capital cannot be accumulated without correlating production relations with an unequal distribution of the social product. The capital-wage relation serves precisely as a medium of surplus value creation, social stratification, and capital accumulation.

Today, the capitalistic evolution of primitive accumulation has reached the stage which we call globalization. With globalization representing the construction of an uneven global economic space decentered from specific national territories. Within this context, the capitalist world system aims to propel itself purely on the surplus created through the capital-wage relation, as people to people relations of domination have yielded an incredible amount of surplus to the capitalist accumulators through the institutions of colonial conquest, slavery, peonage, contract labor, wage slavery, etc.

Over the past 500 years almost all non-European peoples have been incorporated into modern capitalism's expansionist social system and were forced to interact with Europeans along various patterns of super-subordination. This disjuncture of the global economy has lead to the forging and sustainment of multi-stranded social relations that link decentered societies to their points of origin, or transnationalism. Deterritorialized nation state building allows for people to live anywhere in the world and to in a way still not live outside of their nation state of origin through the use of symbols, language, and political and cultural rituals. Transnationals are forced to fundamentally reconceptualize the politics of community, solidarity, identity, and cultural difference. In a world of diasporas, global culture flows, and mass movements of populations, traditional notions of space lose their relevance. Remembered places become the anchors of community for dispersed peoples. The memory of the homeland imaginatively constructs the new land in which one lives. It is within this category that transnationalism develops, the process by which migrants through daily activities, social, economic, and political relations create social fields which cross national boundaries. Thus finding themselves in a situation where nationality or citizenship are not necessarily singular nor exclusive. The categories which imply belonging to a nation, the notions of nationality based on cultural, linguistic, and blood lineage, having legal status, rights, roles, and responsibilities to the society in which one lives become blurred. An ideology that envisions migrants as loyal citizens of their ancestral nation states is constructed in dialectic opposition to the decentralizing goals and tendencies of globalization, while at the same time reflecting globalizing tendencies in that this identity is itself decentered in relation to the transnationals' position in their host society.

3.4 Deterritorialization as a factor which complicates processes of identity formation as group membership among transnationals is determined by traditional views of the nation state. The concept of the nation state is not as weakened by globalization as some would say. Deterritorialization implies the subjectivity of the nation state. Transnationalism has created an individual with conflicting loyalties, living in one place while existing in another.

The process of deterritorialization greatly complicates the processes of identity formation in that as most long term transnationals cannot realistically return to their homeland and as identity is created in a state of extended absence, it may ultimately support rather than conflict with the "official" post-colonial constructs of national identity. Deterritorialised people may also have the tendency to embrace oppressive cultural or ethno-nationalistic projects, a politics of the enactment of grudges against the relatively weak, rather than the pursuit of class or ethnic oppositional politics against national elites which are responsible for those concerned being forced to seek a livelihood abroad. The most common responses to such conditions tend to be rather individualistic in that as solidarities to larger communities are bound by context and are always shifting, a realization occurs that one is obliged to focus on their own interests in a narrow field of immediate family obligations. In all, such an experience can be very diverse, depending on economic returns, gender, and individual experience.

Transnationalism implies the crossing of political borders as well as symbolic borders, connecting the paths of the most divergent spaces of social, economic, and cultural relationships. While on one hand it affords the opportunity to negotiate within this complex structure, it also implies exile, an experience of political marginalization and rightlessness in relation to the homeland which heavily impacts the life and psyche of the transnational. However, the political and economical situation found in the host country produces a situation in which the transnational is simultaneously criminalized by the state as the state consciously fails to regulate the conduct of citizens, and tacitly sanctions a situation in which citizens increasingly vent their frustrations and anxieties on immigrants and those officially stigmatized as the "undeserving poor." Thus comes the realization that the question of who can or should belong and fit into the dominant models of citizenship and social membership are still deeply rooted in the traditional notion of what a nation state is, and that the definition of the nation state in the eyes of the dominant culture has in effect not been as weakened by the processes of globalization as some would like to assume.

At the same time, the concept of deterritorialization implies that the territorial nation state itself is no longer the most significant entity, but rather the cultural narrative that formulates the shape of the nation as according to this logic, wherever the population goes, the nation state goes with them. The nation becomes not a natural nor eternal essence but rather a contingent, slippery, fuzzy construct in a state of constant flux yet with practical implications for people's everyday lives as well as long term political repercussions. Issues concerning the power of the state over individuals, the power relations between employee and employer in relation to the nation state, and the power of the family over individuals, and vice versa, gain new dimensions within this context.

Transnationalism and mass migrations have had the effect of creating a fundamentally new kind of individual, one who is rooted in the space of ideas rather than in temporal space, in memories as much as in the material world. Individuals who are constantly forced to defend themselves because they are defined by "others" through their "otherness." Individuals who have experienced ways of being which depend on a more often than not conflicting experience of where they are, and where they find themselves, people who have crossed a frontier in order to see home.

CHAPTER 4
Constructing the Self

4.0 The universal need to belong.

One of the most profound needs which we all share is to have the knowledge of fundamental belonging. When this need is met, it becomes taken for granted, not even thought about, yet when it is missing, it becomes difficult to fully conceptualize and comprehend. To ponder one's own, or another's identity is not based simply on the desire to know what one is, in contrast to who one is, and the inter-relationship between that "who" and "what," but rather the desire to encounter more individuals like oneself, the desire to confirm that we are not alone, to take part in defining who our kind are, which community we want to associate with, to help shape and confirm our own sense of self.

4.1 Identity as fluid yet constant.

The self is fluid and in process, but determinate at any particular moment, not necessarily hybrid but always complex, determined by experience to a certain extent but at the same time constructed or chosen with varying degrees of awareness, at times defining itself in opposition to others while also in relation to others. Yet at the same time the concept of agency cannot be ignored. Identity is fluid and yet constant as while the defining features of belonging to a group may change over time, what remains as a constant is the very notion of the group itself as existing. The self making process occurs as agency expresses itself within a series of inter-related power relationships which create, legitimate, and constrict each other.

4.2 The notion of boundaries.

Boundaries allow identity to be abstract, in that they allow one to perceive who they are in terms of comparison to others within their own group, but also in contrast to those who are members of other groups. By seeing what one is not, one can attempt to see what one is. Borders can be moral, economic, political, biological, or linguistic, they are flexible and maintained through interactions and negotiations which develop out of the interaction of agency and power within the arena of social constraints. With the creation of boundaries between the public and domestic realms, and the assignment of different values to the products of culturally defined male and female labor, identity also becomes gendered. Because the boundaries of identity are not clear cut, and are in constant flux, individuals can perform various social roles, which may include acts that contradict each other. However, when embraced, various social roles have the potential to coexist, ridding themselves of contradictions. Identity is problematic only when defined within the Western framework of the individual being in opposition to the community rather than in relation to it.

4.3 Identity as a process of being and becoming.

Identity can also be seen as partially being consciously chosen, it becomes a process of being and becoming taking place as we reflect on our constructions of positions in language. We have the ability to situate ourselves in relation to ideas, other individuals, our own culture, other cultures, the universe itself, through the act of linguistically deliberating our position in relation to the world around us. It becomes an ongoing process of self-construction, a subjective array of ongoing processes, never completed, and heterogeneous as it includes the mind as well as body, being simultaneously somatic, psychic, and discursive. The very essential nature of social construction imprisons the self in determination, denying it its freedom. The notion of identity fails to liberate the individual from their subjectification to their language, culture, community, and society.

CHAPTER 5
Language and the Discourse of Becoming

5.0 The role of language in identity formation. Language as the vehicle of cultural expression and group cohesion and solidarity.

While culture, the sum total of ways of living built up by a group of individuals, which is transmitted from one generation to another, is an integral defining feature of culture, it is language which is intrinsic to the expression of culture. As a means of communicating values, beliefs, customs, feelings, and views, it has an important social function which fosters feelings of group identity and solidarity. It is the means through which culture and its traditions, and shared values are conveyed and preserved. Linguistic forms mean nothing in themselves as their meaning is acquired only in their relations to other forms.

5.1 Historical antecedence of language's role in identity formation.

In a historical perspective, a unified language and a stable, unified identity have both been traditionally considered to be necessary for the effective functioning of an individual. Multicultural communication, and transnationalism have however shaken the foundations of such assumptions. Both languages and identities mix and blur boundaries as individuals learn and use different languages and roles as the intersection of needs, desires, intentions, history, and identities calls for. The result of this however is not the chaos once predicted, but rather an acceptance of language and identity to be more complex, flexible, and much less threatened by difference than has been previously assumed.

5.2 Language and the nation state, the concept of national identity.

In the context of the nation state, and defining nationality, while a common language does not make a nation, language does play a fundamental role in the formation of national identity by establishing an invisible national boundary which is less arbitrary than territoriality, while being less exclusive than ethnicity. Language, as the direct expression of culture becomes the bastion of cultural resistance, the last fortress of self control, a refuge of identifiable meaning for its speakers. However, the idea that citizens need a common language to discuss common affairs rests not on the implication that a common language is necessary for understanding, but on the implication that all citizens see things the same way, or come to a consensus on values.

5.3 The state of alienation which comes about due to the conflict between language and identity among minorities. The detrimental effects of linguicism. The English language as not being a neutral element in the United States despite its portrayal as such. Linguistic difference as being parallel to social distance in respect to the prestige culture

A state of alienation exists between language and identity that is established early on in an individual who is not part of the dominant culture, whose language is not that of officialdom. One is taught to develop false speech patterns, to separate the story from the telling of the story, to understand that the telling has more value than the story itself. It is because of this that the majority of white, middle class Americans tend to believe that schools are neutral because their politics and world view are never in question. Being the prestige culture, they do not have to explain why they think as they do, or why they respond as they do. The material circumstances of one's childhood have a strong impact on identity formation. The cultural denial of class memory excludes those whose approach to the world is formed by the experience of disenfranchisement and memories of oppression.

Those who speak a language other than that of the dominant culture internalize how their own language is used against them by the dominant culture, and consequently fall prey to having their own language used against them. Repeated attacks on one's native tongue diminishes their sense of self, as those attacks last one's entire life, the catastrophic outcome can easily be imagined. When one acquires a low estimation of their language, they in effect acquire a low estimation of themselves.

The notion of English as a "neutral" language in a "neutral" education environment is far from being reality as it includes the connotation that difference is not merely the act of being different, but rather stipulates awkwardness, inferiority, and incompleteness in a state of direct opposition to the dominant, prestige culture. A language is revealed as distinctive only when it is viewed in relation to other languages, in that each language then takes on the role of a point of view, of a socio-ideological conceptual system of real social groups and their embodied representatives. As language and ideology are inseparable, with language being representative of a superordinate or a subordinate group, language is not only a marker of ethnicity or nationality, but also of ideology. Xenophobia towards non-English speakers in the United States, or English Only programs represent not only the desire for cultural assimilation, but also the desire to stamp out different ideological currents which are seen as threatening. Within this context, ethnic awareness can be identified as the perception by members of a minority of the social distance separating them from the dominant group and the existence of discrimination. It is such an awareness which leads to alienation, ostracism, and a sense of inferiority that more often than not causes the minority person to defer from the majority. The oppressed minorities tend to carve out spaces of dignity for themselves by making their ethnic borders impermeable. As the human experience is participated in through dialogue, two way, ongoing communication between individuals and communities is necessary in order for equal negotiating powers to be present. The proof of any real acceptance of difference implies the right of the other to participate fully in defining the terms of the dialogue, allowing for culture to be defined through a series of transpositions and translations. The concept of a dialogue becomes a metaphor for the transition between two nations and the dialectical tension between two cultures.

CHAPTER 6

Hispanic Identity: Constructing the Self, Becoming the Other

6.0 An introduction to Hispanics in the United States. A discussion of the term Hispanic and its relevance. The term does not imply the favoring of a colonial identity but rather reflects the processes of creolization which have shaped Latin America.

Perhaps the most visible "other" in the United States today are the 38.8 million inhabitants whose origins lie in the Ibero-American world. An approximate two thirds of these individuals are of Mexican origin, 9% are Puerto Rican, 4% Cuban, and the rest comprising of an amalgam of individuals from nearly 20 other nations. While arguments have been made to stipulate that the term Latin or Latino/a describes this conglomerate of peoples better than the term Hispanic,

I nonetheless choose to use the term Hispanic. Latin refers to the name of the people who founded the Roman Empire, their descendents, and their language, the official language of the Roman Catholic Church, as well as any individual who speaks a language descended from Latin. Thus anyone from any of the French, Spanish, or Portuguese speaking countries of Africa, anyone from Latin America, Portuguese speakers from Macau, Spanish speakers from the Philippines, people of "Latin" ancestry in Goa, and anyone from Spain, Portugal, Italy, France, Belgium, Romania, Andorra, and parts of Switzerland can call themselves Latin. Such a label is too wide and complex to be used merely as a synonym for the amalgam of Spanish speaking peoples and their descendants in the United States. If the label is to be applied, it must be so according to its original meaning, as the collective group of Romance speaking peoples of the world, and the subsequent cultural orientation of those peoples towards the Romance speaking nation states of Europe. Hispanic on the other hand is a much narrower category, and one more fitting to describe the bulk of Ibero-American transnationals in the United States. The label Hispanic implies one who speaks Spanish, or is of descent from the regions of the world which comprise the sphere of Spanish cultural influence.

While it can be argued that the label favors a Spanish colonial heritage, and thus reinforces the colonial legacy, the label Latin does exactly the same thing. However, by using Hispanic to describe Spanish speaking individuals, and their descendants, it does not necessarily mean that a position based on legitimating cultural imperialism, linguistic imperialism, colonialism, or cultural genocide is being made, rather one merely describes the present situation of those cultures and peoples, and the fact remains that even those of non-Spanish ethnic origins have appropriated the Spanish language and aspects of the Spanish cultural and historical legacy, such an observation is merely that, an observation. The label Hispanic does not insinuate that the cultural legacy of the Spanish speaking world is merely a transplant of Spain's culture and language.

On the contrary, any understanding of the colonial history of Latin America calls for the discourse of processes of creolization as such processes offer an alternate option to assimilation or acculturation, which is brought about by the negotiation of two or more peoples in a context where an imbalance of power occurs. This imbalance greatly affects cultural evolution but does not necessarily favor transfer from the prestige culture in all cases. Political, social, and economic power are not the only determinants of cultural selection. One must also examine the situation of the environment, interaction between groups, and the general status of the relationship between the colony and the metropole. Creolization came about due to the asymmetrical power structure of colonial relationships. With stress placed on cultural exchange and synthesis, it could accommodate the demands of global flows in an increasingly capitalist ethos, while at the same time satisfying the needs of the anti-imperial nationalism which seeks an indigenous, common cultural intermixture as its new substructure. Creolization within this context becomes a force which naturalizes cultural combinations. Yet in all of this we find the search for a new native identity erupting from a situation where the perceived group had no true natal society, thus creolization becomes a way of creating stability out of chaos. Perhaps the Cuban scholar Fernando Ortiz stated it best when he referred to creolization as the "constant interaction, the transmutation between two or more cultural components whose unconscious end is the creation of a third cultural whole-that is, culture-new and independent, although its bases, its roots, rest on preceding elements."

6.1 The term Hispanic as a label defining a speech community. The notion of group cohesion based on the ability to communicate effectively.

The label Hispanic does not refer to any notions of biological affinity nor to ethnicity, but rather to a speech community. Divisions in national origin, social class, education level, ethnicity, race, and the such make it difficult to define Spanish speaking transmigrants as a single group as common cultural denominators beyond language are hard to define. The label is nonetheless deficient, but I chose what I perceive to be the lesser of two evils, as any state imposed label which ignores cultural and historical differences and perpetuates an imposed project that culturalizes economic exploitation and political oppression serves no one but the status quo. It must be remembered that the majority of Hispanics are located where they are within the American hierarchy not because of their culture or language, but because of their class location in the economic system. Class location has a lot to do with the terms of one's ethnicity and self perception vis-a-vis "white" Americans, as those Hispanics of middle or upper class origins tend to participate in competitive ethnicity while those from disenfranchised segments of society tend to have the ethnic interface of colonial ethnicity.

The idea of a common speech community implies a group which shares a common basic world view, and is a predisposition to the feelings of kinship which one holds with other Spanish speakers they have never seen. Spanish speakers and their descendants from places as far apart as Argentina and Nicaragua often feel a recognition of themselves in the other, something which they do not experience with non-Hispanics, it is this sense of vague mutual recognition or perhaps even empathy which provides the very foundations for an imagined community. Imagining the new community is made easier through the various easily encountered sources of communication technologies which we are exposed to, television, radio, the internet, online chat programs, and the printed media. Television has proven to be an especially powerful tool in the diffusion of the images of the imagined community, as the viewers of nationally broadcast Spanish language television become parts of a unified audience, learning of the same events and hearing their language spoken in relatively homogenous accents which are perhaps a sign of an emerging North American dialect of Spanish.

6.2 The creation of a common history based on linguistic unity among Hispanics in the United States. This focus on history allows for traditional hierarchies to be recreated as the mind is the locus of discourse and negotiation.

As accents seem to melt together, so does the notion of history, as a common history which emphasizes the common events and conveniently forgets the conflictive ones takes hold in the imagined "Hispanic" nation, or the perceived unified Hispanic population of the United States. Such a common history more often than not focuses on the prestigious literary tradition of the Spanish language, even among those who do not perhaps even speak the language. Such an approach views literary figures such as Cervantes, Mistral, Asturias, Neruda, Paz, and Garcia Marquez as the patrimony of the Hispanic world, rather than of their respective nations and cultures alone. It is a history which focuses on the common political and cultural history of more than 300 years of Spanish colonialism, thus the reason why Columbus Day, or Dia de la Raza(Day of the Spanish Race) is stressed far more among Hispanics in the United States than it is in Latin America. October 12, 1492 represents a mythical starting point of Hispanic commonality as it marks Columbus' arrival in present day Haiti, and the subsequent beginning of the miscegenation of Europeans, Amerindians, and Africans which has lead to the creation of new peoples and cultures. This official mythology however fails to render room for the constant state of warfare and chaos which marked the conquest, and for the later conflicts which erupted between the newly formed nation states which constitute the Hispanic universe. The wars between Chile, Peru, and Bolivia, between Paraguay and Argentina, Uruguay and Brazil, Paraguay and Bolivia, among the Central American republics, and most recently between Ecuador and Peru are ignored. The political tension between those two nations, and between Nicaragua and Costa Rica, Honduras and El Salvador, Colombia and Venezuela, while they help shape perceptions of those respective nations and their people at home, are swept away in the context of the imagined nation, the new homeland.

In a way, such a situation serves to merely reestablish the "traditional" hierarchies of Latin American societies, where by ethnicity it exists in a dual nature. The vast majority of Amerindians, Blacks, and to a lesser degree Mestizos and Mulatos have never ceased to be impoverished and denied true economic, social and political equality with the descendants of the Europeans who settled the region, and continue to dominate, successfully hidden behind the national identities which are based on the values and mores of the prestige, Spanish, cultural elite. The homogenization of Latin America among transnationals in the United States serves as a mode of appropriating elite values. Such a notion parallels the linguistic situation of Latin America, where the more educated one is, the higher their prestige, the more apt they are to use a rather standardized version of the Spanish language, which differs slightly in tone, accent, and some vocabulary from country to country, while the oppressed, non-European elements of society tend to use speech patterns which clearly differentiate them from the elite and the upper middle class. The perpetuation of such a mind set, of such a world view acts to imprison the peoples of Latin America, as well as Hispanics in the United States in an oligarchic, Europeanized, colonized vision. Among Hispanic transnationals, the desire to negate difference behind a fraudulent notion of sameness in effect hides the dehumanization of peoples. It represents the psychic markings on a colonized people that forms part of a discourse which turns history into fiction on the basis of political reality. Language is not an abstract system of normative forms, every word represents the context which socially charges it, and the intentions which give it life. Official narratives such as "documented" events, news items, books, and unofficial narratives such as jokes or gossip express a theoretical self awareness of history and fiction as human constructs created in the matrix of memory, image, and imagination.

6.3 The benefits associated with adhering to a pan-identity.

At the same time, the emergence of a nationalistic, political consciousness benefits the group as collective methods are more apt in overcoming fears, insecurities, and self doubts among those who feel alienated by language, class, and American attitudes towards minorities. Doing things together, acting as a collective has the potential of strengthening confidence in the accessibility of the American political system and can ease the apathetic individual into political awareness by introducing the system in a more familiar social situation. This is best accomplished by bridging the gap between private concerns and public issues. Such political methods are however displayed in a hierarchical structure with which one is familiar.

6.4 Historical antecedents. The notion of a Hispanic pan-identity as rooted in globalizing processes rather than the United States bureaucracy. A look at globalizing processes in Latin America and the consequent anti-globalization currents to arise. The United States' interference in Latin America as a colonial process.

The origins of such a collective consciousness are not in the United States, and do not correlate directly to the labeling of all Spanish speakers and their descendants into the same category by American bureaucrats. Rather, the concept is directly linked to the processes of globalization which have created transnationalism in the first place.

The period between 1900 and 1950 is one of transition for Latin America in that it is marked by United States sponsored investment and political programs aimed at "modernization" through means of industrialization. The period gave rise to a de sarrollista(developmentalist) nationalism among the elite which called for more state sponsored capitalist economic development. Traditional, native ways of life were looked on as "primitive," and the non-European aspects of society, both cultural, as well as those of non-European descent were looked upon as an "embarrassment" to the newly emerging society. It was a period marked by vast urbanization and massive migration flows to the United States. Industrialization, and "modernization" or better said Westernization, brought an extreme amount of wealth to a few, created a small, heavily Westernized, urban middle class, and heightened living standards somewhat for those who negated their non-European heritage, while bringing poverty and repression to the masses.

After a failed experiment with import substitution in the 1960's, Latin American economies became internationalized and more subordinated to the core of the world economy. In the mid 1970's, Latin American economies began to collapse, and in the 1980's the desarrollista illusion crashed. The outcome was a condition of monumental disparities of income and living standards between different classes and ethnic groups.

The present notion of a collective identity arises from these times. The Cuban Revolution was a great achievement as it was seen as standing up to the then already world hegemonic United States. To many people it was a surreal achievement as they saw their own homelands in the grips of dependence on the West, their own people idealizing everything Western, and aspiring to be like the industrial West, while this small island nation stood up for itself and said "no" to world hegemony, and chose its own path towards progress, its own destiny. The message that modernization does not equal Westernization, and that the Cuban nation would openly pursue an alternate path of its own choosing to that chosen for it by the West, shook Latin America and the world.

However, the reaction of the United States and the Western camp was swift. Afraid of losing its "colonies" as the message of the Cuban Revolution spread, Latin America began to experience a wave of United States sponsored ultra-right wing regimes and wars of counterinsurgency. Such policies continue to be a defining feature of United States foreign policy towards Latin America even today. One does not have to look to the past to see this, the U.S. brokered counterinsurgency in Nicaragua, and the open support and financing of the repressive yet pro American government of El Salvador in the 1980's have parallels in the United States' present day support of counter government movements in Venezuela and Cuba, and in the support given to the right wing Colombian government and the counterinsurgency paramilitary forces in that country.

6.5 Hispanic transnationalism as a direct product of the United States' intervention and of globalization. The consequent rise of pan-identity as tool of resistance to globalizing currents. The notion of Hispanic as a state of mind forged in a post-colonial world.

The chaotic large scale intranational and international migratory flows produced by the macro-economic dislocations and the political upheavals caused by such intervention have been a radical factor in the transformation of the identities of large numbers of Latin Americans in that in face of such a perceived threat, an anti-systematic, anti-imperialist, class, cultural, and historical solidarity has reemerged. Such a solidarity, a sense of latinoamericanismo(Latin Amricanism), jump started by the Cuban Revolution, and fueled by the disparities of "modernization" has not been seen since the days of Tupac Amaru or Simon Bolivar. This new identity however is not merely reactive, but also affirmative.

Unfortunately, latinoamericanismo has not yet gone deep enough into the historic consciousness of the continent, an identity glossed over by the wild rush to a "modernity" instrumentalized by both the capitalist accumulators and their anti-systematic opponents into a form of modernity based on the tenets of the colonial legacy. Pan-ethnicities of any type face a deep struggle for life against the ideologies promoted from above by media outlets, state bureaucracies, elites, and the resurgence of nationalism, militarism, hedonism, and consumerism. Conflict also arises with pro-systematic ethnicities manufactured from the top down in order to define pan-ethnicities ahistorically. An example of such a pro-systematic manufactured ethnicity is the government sponsorship of conservative organizations to which officialdom gives the authority to speak on behalf of and represent the Cuban community in Miami. Nonetheless, a legacy for a common Latin American pan-ethnicity has been set in motion by the anti-colonial struggle, and the resistance to the coercive methods of globalization. To view the Hispanic pan-ethnicity merely as a bureaucratic creation of the United States disempowers and negates the legitimacy of Hispanics as a single entity. In the era of diasporas, imperialism, transnationalism, the act of remembering and appropriating a history that has been denied, neglected, or forgotten by colonization or the psychological fractures of relocation, the need to reclaim the site of memory, a space where one seek refuge, an imagined homeland, becomes a political act. The translation of the concepts of nation, identity, ethnicity, community, and group, into a linguistic and even metaphysical idiom turns it into an object of intense reflection, the notion of being Hispanic becomes perceived as a state of mind, as a force of ancestral memory forged by the postcolonial world, or the sense of independence, and struggles of a colonized people, their project of asserting difference from the imperial center, the cultural processes affected by imperialism from the moment of colonization to the present day.

CHAPTER 7
The Mexican Experience

7.0 An introduction to Mexican transnationalism.

The Mexican diaspora constitutes over two thirds of the Hispanic population of the United States, an approximate 25 million individuals, and the largest transnational community in the world. Its experiences vary from those who constitute descendants of the "accidental immigrants," or those who found themselves on the U.S. side of the California and New Mexico borders at the end of the U.S.-Mexican war, the descendants of the first colonizers of Texas, the descendants of the miners and railroad workers who arrived in the United States after the Mexican Revolution, the migrant farmers and workers who continue to arrive in the United States today, and the small number of professionals and intellectuals who seek career opportunities in a new land. The Mexican experience consists of the challenges they face, the changes that occur in them and their children, the affect they have on the United States, and the one the United States has on them, their Mexican legacy, and the affect of their legacy on Mexico. The ways in which they negotiate their world views, legitimate their Mexicanness as a state of mind, as an imaginary space which transcends any temporal or territorial borders, their act of being and becoming Mexican while being an at times feared and unwanted yet integral part of the United States. Furthermore, Mexican transnationalism is a prototype of unidirectional migration, in that 98% of Mexican transmigrants are bound for the United States alone. A situation determined by a history of war and conquest of territory, the existence of a historically fluid border between the two nations. While the numerical predominance of Mexicans among Hispanics may lead one to conclude that an approach to Mexicans alone would be more prudent than a look at Mexicans within the context of Hispanics in general, it must be noted that while they are numerically the largest group, they are also politically the weakest. A factor stemming from the fact that many are illegal immigrants or unskilled workers. Furthermore, the Mexican community is heavily dispersed throughout the United States, and is subsumed in the wider context of Hispanic community in those urban areas where it tends to concentrate. Likewise, the Mexican community shares the same contextual problems and concerns as the wider Hispanic community.

7.1 Motives for transmigration, the processes of choosing where to go and why.

While the decision to go north can be looked at as a flight, or an adventure by some, the reality is far from such notions. Rather than being a decision made as if by the toss of a coin, people go where they have contacts, acquaintances, friends, family, as well as at least rudimentary knowledge of what the place is like. In the journey north, personal considerations turn out to be secondary considerations, and one's tastes or preferences for a certain place over another have next to nothing to do with the choice of destination itself. In terms of the specific destination, the choice depends on the extension and diffusion of the network of relationships that each person has, is restricted to an individual's own social capital in the broadest sense. The choices which are made lack improvisation in that they become reduced to each individual's human and social capital. Thus an urban or agricultural setting is selected according to one's occupation in the homeland. With education, skills, and class determining what position is available to them in the United States, the class hierarchy of the homeland is recreated in the host country and its social constructs consequently become reinforced. As transmigrants tend to move en masse towards given destinations upon arrival, over time the given population tends to acquire or transform its own human and social capital, continuing to disperse from that point which becomes a certain nucleus of origin. More often than not, such a point becomes manifested as an ethnically defined neighborhood. The dispersion pattern rests on two main factors, amount of time in the United States, and the job market, as geographical mobility is directly related to wage improvement in the United States. What is left to fortune and mirrors the toss of a coin within these processes are the conditions and course of events which they encounter upon reaching their destination.

7.2 The historical origins of Mexican transmigration over the last few decades.

The factors which have contributed to the rise of immigration from Mexico in the last few decades finds its origins in the economic policies applied in both Mexico and the United States from the years of the Second World War up to the 1970's as in 1942 the United States set up the Bracero Accord which allowed for the importation of foreign workers. Over the next 22 years, some 4.6 million temporary workers were imported from Mexico. However, when the program ended in 1964, the United States was so indebted to their labor that it could economically simply not function the same without them, so Mexican migrant workers continued to be employed. What happened in reality was simply a policy shift from a policy of active labor recruitment to one of a de facto policy of passive labor acceptance which combined modest legal immigration with massive illegal immigration.

In the 1970's, the economic model was undone and changed into one based on international trade.

In the industrialized world, such a move marked a growth in production as more capital intensive markets fragmented and mass production methods gave way to flexible accumulation, out-sourcing, and continuous flow manufacturing, carried out on a global scale. In the developing world, the change was marked by decentralization and privatization programs, and consequently a greater dependence on and subordination to the West as those nations lacked, and continue to lack the infrastructure to compete on the economic battleground set forth by globalization.

In Mexico, the northern border region was the first to receive the blows of such economic change as in the 1970's the Mexican government launched an industrialization program along the border based on export processing. Agreements were made with the United States which allowed for the creation of a trade zone that allowed American companies to import unfinished products into Mexico, assemble them there, and then export them back to the United States in order to save on paying taxes to the U.S. government. The growth of this industry initiated a rapid wave of demographic growth along the boarder as individuals sought work in the growing "maquila" factories.

Under the presidencies of Miguel de la Madrid and Carlos Salinas de Gortari in the 1980's, this trade agreement was expanded to include all of Mexico. The move was marked by the General Agreement on Tariffs and Trade in 1986, and by the negotiations dealing with the North American Free Trade Agreement which began with the United States and Canada in 1988 and was finally ratified by Mexico on January 1, 1994.

These moves had differing effects in different regions of Mexico, along the northern frontier, cities such as Tijuana, Mexicali, Ciudad Juarez, Nuevo Laredo, and Monterrey heavily expanded while cities in the center and south of the country found themselves sinking into despair as they were unable to compete in the global market. It is for this reason that the neoliberal policies of president Carlos Salinas de Gortari have left Mexico a legacy of increased unemployment, hardships, neglect, and an alarming rate of growing economic marginalization. For the newly disenfranchised, such dire despair left many with little or no choices, namely to either revolt or emigrate. Thus the first armed revolt in Mexico since the early 1940's occurred in Chiapas, a pervasively poor, predominantly rural, highly marginalized, heavily Indigenous populated state. Without social ties connecting residents to work opportunities abroad, and no real history nor tradition of migration, the most feasible option for the Chiapanecos was rebellion. However, in states such as Guerrero, Michoacan, and Oaxaca, which have traditions of migration to the United States, sporadic guerrilla movements emerged but were never consolidated into mass uprisings as the remittances sent from abroad mitigated the pressures for revolt and circumscribed the appeal of armed rebellion.

7.3 The effects of globalization on the United States over the last few decades.

The expansion of the global economy also had some serious consequences for the destination of Mexican transnationals. After the early 1970's, wages in the United States stagnated, unemployment grew, and the gaps between classes rose. During the 1970's and the 1980's, economic insecurities were mainly the concerns of the blue collar workers, while by the early 1990's, the same fears swept through the white collar world as a cyclical recession was triggered by the end of the Cold War. The combination of rising income inequality, stagnating wages, and a rising immigration rate created a situation of excessive social tensions.

7.4 The border as a source of conflict, both physical as well as symbolic. Conflict as expanding from this region along with a transnational presence.

The conflict between individuals and nation states enacted along the United States-Mexico border, and which has by now expanded into the very hearts of both nations and peoples, serves as a dramatization of the growing challenge of engaging the mass movement of people, their ideas, products, institutions, cultures, the arena for defining their values and allocating their resources. It destabilizes ideas of community, culture, nationality, and the territorial nation itself as being fixed and unitary.

This conflict can be seen beyond the border as both the United States of America as well as the United States of Mexico constructed narratives to position themselves in the nation-centered nineteenth and twentieth centuries. Both Americans and Mexicans looked towards the country of the "other" as both defined their history and traditions in direct opposition to each other. With the United States historically seeing Mexico as a cultural threat and a roadblock to the western expansion of the American Empire, and Mexico seeing the United States as an imperialist enemy, occupying over half of Mexican territory. After the Mexican Revolution, Mexico and the United States represented two very different national models which exist in dialectic opposition to each other, one of a nationalism based on the first twentieth century social revolution, and the other on the most resilient capitalist economy in the world. Yet with the Americanizing of culture, the introduction of consumerism to replace Mexican ideals, the sense of history becomes a tale of tragedy. A tragedy symbolized by the ascendance of Los Angeles over Mexico City as a new mecca for Mexican life, people, and culture for many. Transnationals have created a border that instead of being a line separating two distinct entities on a map, is a border in which national narratives are less important than the processes of intimate relationships. At the same time there are fears in the United states as the Mexican population in the country has tripled since 1970, and the border region has become heavily Mexicanized or Hispanicized as the growth of that population has been concentrated in the border states. An outcome of this fear includes the passing of California's Proposition 187 and other similar anti-immigrant measures elsewhere in the country.

7.5 Historical antecedents of present day tension along the border. The Historical processes involved in the shaping of the first Mexican-Americans due to physical shifts in the border, and the appearance of the first transnationals due to the American conquest of northern Mexico.

The recent tensions in the region are however not unique. As the United States conquered the northern half of Mexico in 1848, the first group of Hispanics in the United States, the first Mexican-Americans, were confronted with widespread discrimination that greatly diminished their ability to exercise their rights, despite having received United States citizenship. Faced with racism and the position of being a conquered demoralized people, Mexicans of all classes gradually slid lower and lower in the economic ladder and were compelled to devise a variety of new subject positions in reaction to their new political status and changing material conditions in the United States. The dwindling caste of those with sufficient material means and sufficiently light skin had the option of professing to be Spanish in order to lay claim to a type of whiteness, which although not as esteemed as that of the Anglo elite, put those individuals in a better social position than their darker skinned, Indigenous featured kin. For most, phenotypical markers, lower class standing, a lack of proficiency in English, and increasing spatial segregation combined to militate against even the most basic forms of social integration into United States society. The mutually perceived lines of difference sharpened over the course of the nineteenth century as American expansion into the occupied territory grew.

In response to the increasingly negative experiences the Mexicans faced, they were forced to develop new mechanisms of adaptation, mechanisms which drew on sources of collective identity and solidarity only broadly related to notions of formal nationality or citizenship. Being separated from Mexico, however unwillingly, and blocked in virtually every venue from achieving meaningful integration in the social, political, and economic structures being juxtaposed on their lives by the American settlers, Mexicans were forced into the unsettled margins of society. Faced with territorial encroachment and cultural hostility, isolation from both the dominant national and cultural systems of Mexico as well as the United States, they were forced to mediate their profound sentiments of displacement, and other stresses of daily existence as members of a racialized and marginalized minority it a region they had always considered to be their ancestral homeland.

They found themselves immigrants without ever having emigrated from their homes. A new nation was thrust upon them without any consent, leaving them to negotiate their world view and find solace in a nation which now existed in a third space. Thus Mexico existed as an imagined homeland for these first "accidental immigrants," as what was, soon existed only in memory. To understand the notions of difference which exist between Mexicans and Americans, and the significance of the northern border for Mexico, and the power of the imagined homeland over migrant populations, this monumental episode of the Mexican historical narrative cannot be ignored.

The dynamics of the border region became even more complicated as the Mexican Revolution began in 1910. As the social and class polarization created by economic development on both sides of the border converged with the political upheaval in Mexico, the resulting chaos contributed to the shattering of existing senses of collective identity and nationality and the creation of a range of new ones for people throughout Mexico as well as Mexicans in the United States. In reaction to the Mexican Revolution, the United States enacted Americanization programs for Mexicans towards the end of the First World War. Such measures focused on the policing and disciplining of Mexicans in order to ensure the most efficient exploitation of their labor, they were seen as a way of managing what was commonly referred to as the "Mexican Problem" in the southwestern United States. In reality, many could not see Mexicans as a part of United States civic culture, therefore Americanizing measures were designed as a way to ensure the orderly control of a group of people believed by mainstream culture to be racially inferior and suited for little more than cheap labor.

7.5.1 The reaction of Mexican officialdom to the border conflict. The tension which ensued due to the convergence of Mexican sponsored strategies of resistance and the American assimilationist agenda.

In reaction to such measures, the Mexican government, in accordance with its precepts of mexicanismo, of being Mexican, defending the Mexican Revolution as a symbol of sovereignty, cultural and moral values, and an embodiment of the Mexican people, set up a series of consulates which served to help protect the rights of the Mexican population in the United States. The term Mexico de afuera, or Mexico abroad, for the migrant population echoes with a resounding memory of the fact that the land they inhabited was in fact once an integral territorial part of the Mexican nation, but more importantly that it still remains a part of that nation in a moral, cultural, imagined sense. By promoting youth soccer leagues, patriotic and honorific committees, 16th of September and May 5th celebrations, allegiances to Mexico are fostered, as well as an official Mexican presence in "Greater Mexico."

However, such measures were not welcomed by all Mexicans in the United States. For members of the small, upwardly mobile bourgeois sectors of Mexican transnationals, as well as those of Mexican descent who have been assimilated, immigration was widely viewed as a threat. Consequently, in border cities such as Brownsville, Corpus Christi, Laredo, San Antonio, El Paso, Tucson, and Los Angeles, Mexican elites complained of new transnationals competing directly with those already established there for jobs and housing. Yet even though they agreed on such measures, there was heavy disagreement concerning their own national orientations and political agendas.

7.6 The historical legacy of conflict as reflected in the state of present day transnationals and the innovations which have arisen from such antecedents.

The legacy of these ongoing historical processes consequently affects the majority of the working class ethnic Mexicans in the United States. They are thus compelled to operate in those unstable, interstitial social spaces that were by nature separate worlds of cultural and social syncretism and experimentation. Under such conditions, one is much more likely to have a flexible and highly instrumentalist sense of identity regarding national affiliation, as concerns of economic survival and the maintenance of familiar everyday practices outweigh the concerns of the political and historical narratives of the nation state. Yet the persistence of an identity, or an emic designation of Mexican, the notion of Mexicanness as a state of mind is allowed to flourish due to the segregated nature of the urban barrios and rural enclaves. The preservation of familial and religious festivities, entertainment, and other forms of expressive culture keep Mexican culture alive, as well as allow for the Spanish language to flourish. However, as transmigrants from various regions of Mexico, as well as from other parts of Latin America traverse through the various barrios and colonias, the contact made between them allows for the notions of nationality, community, forms of collective as well as individual identity to be blurred and become subject to constant mutation and recombination. Such a literal fluidity of populations in the barrios and colonias promotes the fluidity of identity in that these dynamic social spaces compel and encourage the development of new forms of social knowledge and cultural innovation, invigorating the already present enclaves, which in turn lay down the foundations for and allow for the emergence of alternate and sometimes oppositional forms of discourse. Namely the movement in a sociocultural milieu marked by a Mexican ethnic infrastructure, Spanish language media, small businesses, clubs, restaurants, sports leagues, and the such, which while patterned on those found in the homeland, have been reformulated to conform to the needs of individuals from various parts of the homeland with which one would otherwise not have contact were it not for their state of transmigration.

7.7 The creation of new social spaces by Mexicans.

At the same time, these conditions which express Mexican culture, and allow for the strengthening of the image of the imagined homeland, also allow for the ability to live in an alternative social space that has little to do with formal Mexican citizenship status more comfortable. The following of largely autonomous cultural practices in the new social spaces which are literally situated between the state centered national systems of the United States and Mexico allow for the flexibility to move in a social world that runs counter to both larger societies. However, a consequence of such an existence, a virtual state of statelessness, is the lack of political power in both the homeland and the host country. Thus arises the inability to change the conditions at home which made transmigration a necessity, as well as the inability to realistically challenge the lack of rights and exploitation encountered in the host country. The awareness of their economic displacement and political alienation in Mexico and of their experience of racial discrimination and exploitation in the United States has created a deep sense of ambivalence and cynicism among working class Mexicans to both national systems. As a result of the multiple layers of alienation, new forms of consciousness based on alternative senses of affiliation such as Native Americans, workers, women, Chicanos, homosexuals, now compete with nationality as a primary category of self identification. In the face of a constant decrease of skilled blue collar jobs, and the failure of the public education system to meet the needs of bilingual students, such new senses of identity and orientation serve to further alienate Hispanics in general from mainstream society, symbolizing the rejection of integration into a system which they perceive as not meeting their most basic needs. The myth of the melting pot, which promises vertical social mobility based on individual merit in a classless society does not explain why Mexican immigrants remain at the bottom of the social pyramid when it comes to levels of education and income. The effects of marginalization on identity formation, of being in a position where one's group is commonly known as that with the lowest level of education, the least social prestige, are detrimental to say the least.

7.8 The socio-economically upwardly mobile minority of Mexican transmigrants as both Hispanic and American.

However, for the small upwardly mobile segment of the Mexican transmigrant population, the story is a bit different as through the acceptance of the pan-ethnic identity of being Hispanic, they are able to take part in what can be termed a cultural renaissance in terms of the development of a new Hispanic cosmopolitan aesthetic. An aesthetic which includes the promotion and celebration of cultural forms and practices including literature, film, art, music, criticism, intellectual endeavors, community activism, and the creation of an "ethnic market" which seeks to spread a generalized, almost homogenized, Hispanic popular culture to the masses. In such ways, the Mexican middle class is allowed to experiment with alternate cultural paths enabled by the social transformation of borders. Given such conditions, the emergence of new forms of self identification, collective identity, and national affiliation are obvious. All in all however, the tradition of continuing to define themselves in ways which mitigate against their cultural assimilation and political socialization as "Americans" remains intact.

7.9 The value placed upon the Hispanic pan-identity by Mexican transnationals and the pragmatics of power and discourse involved.

However, for both segments of the Mexican transnational community, the pan-ethnic identity of being Hispanic, which encompasses both their Mexicanness as well as their solidarity with transmigrants from other Spanish speaking countries is seen as being a vital, advantageous resource. In that it allows for a stronger voice within the United States system, as it recognizes ethnic groups as valid categories through which to express grievances. Thus social, cultural, intellectual, and political mobilization is conducted on the basis of the identity which shows the most promise for rewards. Simply put, there is strength in numbers, the Spanish speaking community and their descendants as a whole have a much better chance of negotiating their position within the structure of the state and the dominant culture, than each ethnicity alone. The pan-ethnic category however does not threaten the distinctive identities of its constituent groups. Self awareness, and defining oneself in opposition to the other within the pan-ethnicity remain a prominent factor. The perpetuation of segregated communities and a series of cultural processes which create an imagined homeland for each group allow for the maintenance and perpetuation of ethnic identity. The pan-ethnicity in effect helps to preserve the individuality of the groups in that it acts as a united front against the discrimination which immigrants as a whole face. It raises self esteem as it defines difference from the dominant culture as a source of strength, it becomes a source of resistance and ethnic solidarity in combating marginality and scant expectations of upward mobility.

7.10   Social spaces, the conflicts and contradictions of life in the imagined homeland. The alienation associated with feelings of not belonging fully to neither homeland nor host country. The conceptualization of the imagined homeland through nostalgia without memory.

Living in social spaces transformed by such trends, and in physically segregated communities, both sides of the border are straddled as the notion of transnational social networks comes into play. For many, a physical border does not exist as social ties and familial obligations bind a person to their place of origin as business affairs, remittances, funerals, weddings, baptisms, and other rites of passage and cultural life inextricably link an individual to the homeland. At the same time, a struggle ensues between belonging to the homeland and being obligationally bound to the host country via economic necessity and the raising of one's family within the new social space. One is stigmatized by the negative stereotype which mainstream thought associates with Mexicans, or Hispanics in general, and yet often times faces social setbacks for being successful with the frameworks of the mainstream culture of the United States.

This alienation, sense of statelessness, belonging to both nation states yet fully to neither, permeates one's world view and shapes the memories of a place left behind, yet taken with them to the United States. Memory allows for reconnection with the space left behind, and allows for the recovery of happiness and balance within one's own life. By being in opposition with the daily reality of alienation, the imagined homeland becomes a beacon of hope and sanity.

The homeland becomes idealized and personalized, it leaves the realm of politics, economy, and struggle, to become a place associated with family, friends, the perceived innocence of childhood, the natural and human-made beauty of the landscape. This reflects the desire for the ideal, an opposition to reality, a defensive mechanism which allows for escape from the struggles and power plays of every day life. The personalized images are further expanded to include the Mexican nation as a collective whole, and in some instances, in the United States, the Mexican nation is viewed as a small part of a perceived collective Hispanic "nation." The feelings and sentiments associated with the images of family and friends are juxtaposed upon the images of buildings, streets, lakes, and the nation in general. The political situation of Mexico, social problems, class and economic struggles, and the unattractive traits of certain individuals do not figure in the mythological memory of the homeland. The creation of a third space in which Mexicans, and Hispanics in general live, allows for this connection to the homeland, for this memory and mythology to be relevant. It creates a situation in which political and geographical borders are no longer valid, while at the same time strengthening collective identity by allowing for greater group cohesion, and consequently the preservation of one's own language and thus culture.

7.10.1 Contradictions and the quest for legitimacy, conflict between the homeland as is and the imagined homeland. The role of language as an identity marker which allows for a claim to legitimacy.

The concept of being a stranger also permeates this relationship however, when ties to the homeland other than nostalgia are brought into play, feelings of disconnection arise as one questions the validity of their connection to the homeland. By having left the homeland, having subtracted one's presence from Mexican society, the issue of whether one has a legitimate claim to Mexican society haunts the diasporic mind. While this mind set contradicts the role of the imagined homeland as a place of comfort, escape, and belonging, it does reinforce the notion of the myth of return to the homeland. The creation of a link to the actual society of Mexico, even when in the form of contradictory imagery, reinforces the validity of that imagery in that it gives it a perceived purpose. The purpose is legitimated by the view that as long as certain ties to the homeland, whether imaginary or not, can be maintained, so can the perceived notion of a legitimate claim to that homeland.

Language becomes a key in the claim to legitimacy, knowledge of the Spanish language is the main tool in transcending the border between American and Mexican society. To be able to speak the language, translates into the ability to be able to communicate with one's conspecifics, the potential ability to belong to Mexican society, while also legitimating one's claim to membership in the larger Hispanic community, as that in itself is defined as a speech community more than anything else. The comprehension of a language represents the ability to cross the border between two abstract political and cultural entities. It requires one to negotiate two worlds, reconcile two allegiances. It is the creation of two facades, two personalities, which one chooses to use in specific conditions for one's benefit, as the ability to blend in linguistically and thus culturally does not cause others to question allegiance. The ability to preserve and speak the Spanish language represents an image of identity which one chooses to present to oneself, to another individual, to a country, people, or community. It represents a move in which one goes from being to becoming. A move in which change becomes the prototype for life.

7.10.2 Conflicts and contradictions arising from the transition to an English speaking world. The conflict between two languages in contact.

The transition to an English speaking world is for many the most difficult aspect of living in a foreign land. The transition from a Spanish speaking world to an English speaking one is difficult as when a language changes, so does the symbolism of its words, and consequently the ideas which those symbols express. While words and grammar can be learned, the expression of emotions, and the symbolism of one's native cosmology cannot be adequately performed in a second language. While Mexicans, or Hispanics in general, may become very proficient in English, the notion that they feel lost, and in a way alienated from United States society by knowing English is ever present. As Spanish is the language in which one is taught to feel, to express their emotional needs in, one finds themselves being less emotional in their daily dealings in English. This consequently makes Americans view them differently than other Hispanics would. For the individual, this symbolically creates a border between the two worlds in which they live. A contradiction arises between the traditional value placed on the Spanish language and the values of the prestige culture of the host country. Within the context of identity formation, it must be noted that language acts as a primary signifier, it serves as a connection to a past which has in an idealized form become a part of one's subconscious. Language allows for nostalgia without memory, as it is the medium of communicating culture, and explaining the symbolism behind it.

7.10.3 The Spanish language as a force legitimating the imagined homeland.

While the Spanish language expresses the ideal, the image of Mexico where comfort and belonging are found, issues which contradict this construction are distanced from Mexican culture and are placed in a more neutral, less emotional position. In this way, the idealized homeland is further legitimated in that it becomes further distanced from issues which would cause the notion of discomfort. As one's perceptions of the homeland are dynamic, contradictions arise as while culturally the image of the homeland remains Mexican, more often than not, the positive values associated with the desire for a better life, the perception of the imagined positive values associated with the benefits of transmigration, become a desire for the homeland. In this manner, views between the two worlds are not simply exchanged or replaced, but rather they are interwoven.

7.10.4 The manifestation of nostalgia without memory and the notion of the myth of return as an attempt to legitimize it. The imagined homeland and nostalgia without memory as aiding and enhancing the position of language as an identity marker.

The celebration and remembrance of the 5th of May, the 16th of September, and Epiphany, events which do not figure in U.S. cosmology, form a large part of the nostalgic view of the homeland. The celebration of such rituals serves to bind an individual to the homeland. They serve as an excuse to reminisce about the homeland, to make phone calls, send greetings; it is a safe context within which to legitimate one's ties to the homeland under the pretense of "ethnic" celebration. Yet the lack of a real social context in which the ritual attains authenticity, in which it makes sense, becomes a measure of the growing distance from the context in which it all does make sense and comes together, while also measuring the falling into place within one's new spatial location. Holidays allow for the practice of nostalgia within a context of defiance to the hegemony of the host country by allowing for the organizing of temporal space as is done in the homeland. Such notions promote the belief that no matter how detached one is physically from Mexico, they can remain Mexican. The nation state leaves the realm of being a geographic and political entity, and turns into one which lives in the minds of its people. The diaspora, the transnational community, becomes a microcosm of the Mexican nation via the concept of the imagined homeland.

Such a perceived connection to the homeland, which to the transnational community is viewed as a dynamic relationship coexisting with the lives of those who remain in the homeland creates a situation which feeds the myth of return. Transnational communities are marked by a yearning to return to their perceived homelands, and create a whole mythology around the notion. Within the transnational experience, the yearning for return, the yearning to escape social alienation, the image of a space which is the only place where one truly belongs, greatly shape identity. Yet the community itself can only exist as long as the myth of return remains unfulfilled. Distance from the homeland acts as an agent without which the homeland, as known by the transnational community, would not exist. The duration of the myth however rests on the realistic possibilities of actually returning to the homeland. For many, while the homeland is mythologically attainable, realistically the chances for return are small. For Hispanics raised abroad, the political and socio-economic conditions of their nations vary so greatly from their imagined view of the homeland, and they have adapted so many features of their host culture, that returning would be like entering an alien world. While for those who have left in search of educational or professional advancement, their leaving was without the intent to return permanently, many however do maintain contacts through visits. Yet for all groups, the myth of return psychologically fulfills their desire to legitimate their belonging to the homeland, to construct their identity as Mexicans. This is perhaps the most profound aspect of defining transnational identity.

Memory fills the absence created by separation from the intellectual, temporal, and physical world know as Mexico. The collection of images one maintains of the homeland is reorganized to better explain one's position within their context. Every image symbolically becomes more important than it actually is, with the goal being to consciously preserve one's happiness and sanity, to legitimate their existence and belonging to the homeland. By creating an image of an entity, no matter how far physically removed, where one belongs, and one which is yearned for, the power of alienation is lessened. Or perhaps only temporarily ignored as the individual escapes into the confines of imagery of their point of origin. The strength of the image of the homeland fosters an understanding of its language, the ability to negotiate daily existence within its confines, and allows one to internalize its structures of power and intimacy. Yet at the same time it must be noted that memory is consciously filtered.

7.10.5 The construct of the imagined homeland as a defense mechanism.

The construction of an imagined homeland, made up of carefully chosen images, and an even more careful interpretation of them, serves as a defense mechanism. A measure that comes about through a realization that becomes clear over time. As one negotiates their existence in a space where they are not endowed with a sense of belonging, they resort to the selective memories of a space where they feel that they do belong. Ultimately, this space takes on mythical proportions, and as such can exist only in a reterritorialized state. The construction of an attainable homeland, of a myth of return, comes about from the ultimate realization that to fully return to the homeland is not possible. If it were, the myth would not be necessary. However, because the world is less than ideal, the imagined homeland does serve a purpose as it allows for the preservation of a Mexican identity in its constituents, and acts as a support construct for one's notion of a sense of identity and belonging.

7.10.6 The contradictions which arise due to the concept of the imagined homeland and nostalgia without memory.

As is the case with all innovations however, there are also consequences. Namely, the added contradictions which make negotiating in the host society less smooth, and that one becomes blinded by sentiments which distance them from a rational view of the homeland, as well as to how one views themselves within the context of the host society. The notions of alienation and being a stranger are so internalized, that one truly does find themselves a stranger in their world. As a remedy, one finds themselves suffering from a nostalgia which idealizes a past that never was, and a dream about a return that will never be. When given the opportunity to negotiate the manners and processes of two nation states, the potential exists to become what one chooses, rather than to merely be what history or accident of geography deems. The unique position of the transnational identity allows one to bridge the homeland and the host land, while belonging wholly to neither, thus constructing an identity which those on either side of the very real border cannot fully comprehend.

PART II.

Mexican Transnationals in Las Vegas:
A Theoretical Model in Action.

CHAPTER 8
Commencing the Project

8.0 An introduction

Having completed my theoretical model, I set out to apply it. As the fastest growing city in the nation, having grown by 85.2% between 1990 and 2000, and with a population of 1.5 million, out of which some 300,000 are of Hispanic origin, the greater Las Vegas area presented itself as an ideal and up to the time of this project, virgin

territory for such research.

CHAPTER 9
Contemplating the Other Las Vegas

9.0 A physical description of the region of North Las Vegas known as "Little Mexico."

As I sat there on the bus, watching the geographical and ethnic landscape change right before my very eyes, I came to realize that the cliche, "the grass is no more greener on the other side," is at times far from true, as I saw the grass become less green before my very eyes, both literally, as well as metaphorically for the overall social landscape of this third world nation in the heart of "Fabulous Las Vegas, Nevada." Moving northwards along Eastern Avenue, the landscape changes immensely upon approaching Bonanza Road, slowly, the geography changes from one of neatly trimmed, landscaped streets, many highlighted by the greenery which is such a precious commodity in this desert, of carefully looked after properties and islands of new economic activity, to a region marred by unkept properties, many being merely shadows of their once middle class existence. A region where the grass is no longer green but a dreary yellowish white, and the trees seem to be slowly suffocating, waning, only their size and the age of the neighborhoods giving any insight as to their former glory and the knowledge which they hide within.

9.1 Describing the ethnoscape.

Likewise, the human landscape mirrors the environmental one, as the bus progresses further north, the faces become different, as the landscape outside the window begins to bear the evidence of the apparent state of poverty which marks the neighborhood, the faces inside and outside begin to exhibit a deeper shade of brown, with weary, desperate, stoic eyes, reflecting the poverty and coldness of the world which they encounter. A sense of "difference," and the notion of "other" leave the realm of theory and become daily practice. For a moment, the bus represents a microcosm of society as the few white faces begin to scramble, attempting to avoid any real eye contact, and form of social interaction with the brown faces with whom they share their ride. The elderly white woman carefully clutches her purse as a group of young Hispanic men board the bus, while the teenage mother holds her infant son and stares aimlessly outside the window at the poverty ridden streets which she calls home, only to be looked at with spite and disapproval by the few non-Hispanic individuals on this journey, and as nothing more than an object by the young Hispanic men who seem to make up the majority of the passengers.

9.2 A changing world, language as defining and redefining reality.

As the bus moves further along, another change in the landscape becomes apparent, the English speaking world is being left behind, "America" now slowly becomes "América." While the names of the streets, Owens, Tulip Lane, Washington, remind us we are still in the United States, the very flavor of those streets seems to be a world away. The presence of supermarkets slowly gives way to small shops marked "panadería," "carnicería," while those few which do remain tend to offer products different from those in the same stores in other parts of the valley. The Albertson's on the corner of Bonanza and Eastern not only offers bilingual service, two entire aisles of canned tropical fruits and beans, raw sugarcane, corn husks, banana leaves, and every type of banana from the common "plátano", to the "plátano maduro" and the "plátano burro," all served up while the store's sound system is tuned in to one of the local Spanish language radio stations. Yet the store serves up something else which the Hispanic population of Las Vegas has apparently become used to, neglect. The store is far less hygienic than other Albertson's locations, with wilted produce on the floors, a black residue marking the floor near the doors, uncleaned spills in the aisles, while two armed security guards roam the premises and parking lot, yet do nothing to even attempt to stop the loitering, and drug deals which occur in plain day light. It is important to note that such activities observed were not relegated solely to Hispanics, on the contrary, the drug business in front of this store seems to be the only fully integrated business in the community.

9.3 Urban renewal and aid from the Mexican government in action.

The one gem of urban renewal in the surrounding area is Escobedo Plaza, a small, new complex built just off the intersection of Bonanza and Eastern, next to Tulip Lane and the Cabana Park apartment complex. The plaza offers services which are in great need and demand in the community, including a health clinic and a legal clinic which charge on a very wide sliding scale, depending on what one can afford to pay. Other services offered include an Alcoholics Anonymous meeting room, a center with free internet service and free weekly computer classes for the community, a free literacy center, and a few businesses whose rent seems to pay for the services offered. Although the area where these services are offered is small, the cleanliness of the plaza, and the landscaping make it a site which the community can be proud of. While it is in no way able to accommodate the needs of the entire community, it does provide a symbolic representation of what the area could become if sufficient funds and caring professionals were available. I later learned that the Mexican Patriotic Committee, an organization promoted by, and which heavily relies on the aid and support of the Mexican government, is responsible for the construction of the complex and the maintenance of the services offered.

9.4 Social spaces and contact. Material aspects of constructing a Hispanic pan-identity.

As one moves along, McDonald's and Jack in the Box slowly give way or stand near empty as small outposts of Mexico and Central America with colorful names such as "El Borrego de Oro," "El Tenampa," and "El Triunfo" bustle with as much nostalgia as they do with activity. While each such establishment professes to be "authentic," the dynamics of culture change are ever present as each restaurants attempts to accommodate both the natives of the same place as the proprietors, as well as the changing tastes of the "colonia" due to culture contact. For example, the pupusa, a Central American corn meal patty stuffed with any combination of cheese, bean paste, bits of fried pork fat, and a leafy vegetable known as "lorroco," is offered on the menus of Mexican restaurants, mostly specializing in the cuisine of the Mexican state of Michoacan. While both the Central American as well as Mexican restaurants in the area, have a tendency to present tamales both of the Mexican as well as Central American variety on their menus. With the difference being mainly in the choice of filling and the use of corn husks versus banana leaves in which to steam them. The "pupusa" and the "tamal" as such represent more than the accommodation of different tastes, they represent the fusion of the American continent, and in effect the bridging of the Hispanic world, the meeting of Mexico and Central America, a very earthly example of the consequence of the forming of the pan-identity of "Hispanic" in the United States. Likewise, the decor of such establishments, while attempting to remain Mexican through the presence of murals and folk art reminiscent of the nationalistic frescoes of the Mexican Revolution, also blends "Hispanic" iconography into the picture. Namely through the presence of portraits of Our Lady of Guadalupe portrayed as the "Empress of the Americas," as well as portraits of Our Lord, Savior of the World, the patron saint of El Salvador, and a popular figure throughout Central America. Two very provincial symbols, nationalistic ones, are portrayed within a context as being the property of one's linguistic conspecifics as well. The internationalization of these symbols serves as a way in which to neutralize the potential for conflict which marks culture contact. While seemingly insignificant, such small elements offer an insight into the effects of culture change, and the reshaping of identity on the simplest of levels. Such actions demonstrate the conscious recognition of change, or contact with the other, of the need for cooperation and compromise, while at the same time understanding that the other in this case, is not so different from oneself. This construction of solidarity and sameness within the image of the other is possible only through the realization of an even more different, more removed "other," namely the English speaking world.

9.5 Aspects of material culture supportive of the notion of the myth of return.

Other businesses in the community are also organized around the consciousness of an identity which goes beyond nationality, which seeks "authenticity" through nostalgia, yet a nostalgia without memory as the image of what the homeland should or could be is depicted, while in actuality the motions of culture change and culture contact are in place. Service related establishments such as notary services for example are marked by the presence of images depicting scenes of the country of origin of the proprietor, yet at the same time are marked by a ubiquitous display of latinoamericanismo through the presence of an array of Latin American flags. At times this display is merely an advertisement for phone cards with special rates for Latin America, while at other times it consists of actual banners. Nonetheless, the display is always prominently placed to demonstrate the establishment's solidarity with conspecifics sharing the Hispanic pan-identity, while at the same time allowing for a public display of connectedness to the homeland, an advertisement that a link still exists, and a substantiation of the transnationals' belief that the stay in the host country is only temporary. As far as a symbolic link can be maintained with the homeland, one can still lay claim to it. Like appeals are made within the goods sector, as products from various Spanish speaking nations, or which appeal to certain tastes are displayed in a manner which emphasizes the variety of tastes which the establishment attempts to accommodate, yet does so under the umbrella of a notion of Hispanic solidarity.

9.6 Manifestations of a marked linguistic hierarchy.

A marked feature of Hispanic owned businesses, and one which is perhaps often overlooked is the presence of a linguistic hierarchy. Upon first entering such establishments, the first thing noticed is the music, generally a Spanish language radio station is tuned into, offering a generic mix of music which is unrelated except for the fact that the songs are in Spanish and are neatly packaged under the label of "Latin" music. Again, the very first introduction one has to the establishment is that of an element which solidifies the Hispanic pan-identity, the notion of a greater pan-ethnicity. The second feature which is encountered is the extent to which the employees and proprietors are bilingual. The inside dynamics of the Hispanic community mirror those of the outside world as well. Namely that the greater one's ability to assimilate to the institutions and constructs of mainstream society, of non-Hispanic Euro-American English speaking society, the better the potential of making it. It then becomes no surprise to notice that the more complex or specialized the service offered is, the more the proprietor and employees are removed from the Spanish speaking world, at times speaking with a broken Spanish and at other times relying on Spanish speaking employees for translation purposes in dealing with the general public. With the goods industry, the pattern is the same in that the more expensive the goods being sold, the less the Spanish speaking ability of the proprietors, when it comes to expensive items such as evening wear, electronics, and expensive jewelry, the owners of such establishments in the neighborhood are Korean.

9.7 Conflict based on class and ethnic differences. Inter-ethnic communication as dictated by necessity.

Some of the non-Hispanic businesses unfortunately take a view of the Hispanic community which lacks social consciousness. One of the most common features of the indoor swap meets which dot the community is the presence of Korean vendors selling bandanas, name brand athletic shoes, and Dickies brand work clothes, in colors associated with the gangs in the area. Such operations are basically legal outfitters for street gangs.

Interactions between the Korean businesses and the Hispanic clientele, or between Spanish speaking and non Spanish speaking individuals within the business context takes place in various forms. From broken Spanish and broken English to a peculiar Spanish-Korean "pidgin" which seems to be basic Spanish terms put into Korean syntax, to blank, awkward stares and a simple looking at the price and exchanging the product for money.

9.8 Common language and cultural features as being definitive of group boundaries as well as of social distance from the prestige culture.

Outside of the business context, human interaction varies. After seeing the apparent appeal of a pan- identity within the economic sector of the community, I was prone to believe that the basis of a sense of community in "Little Mexico" would be a sense of class solidarity rather than ethnicity as such. However, this appears to be only one aspect of the situation as the interaction between the non-Hispanic Euro-American population and the African-American population seems to be pretty fluid and regular, as is the interaction between various Hispanic groups, namely Mexicans, Salvadorians, Hondurans, and Guatemalans. The interaction between the English speaking and the non English speaking peoples is much colder in that it is simply uncommon in the public sphere. This seems to be the case with the somewhat considerable Asian community in the area as well, as the relations between the Philippine and Laotian community and the English speaking world tend to mirror the relations between Hispanic and mainstream American society. While class is an important factor in the solidarity expressed within groups, it is linguistic and common cultural features which are more defining of the community to the outside world. The lack of interaction can be accredited to several factors, while racist tendencies in all parties cannot be fully ignored, I believe the main factor affecting intra group communication to be simply a product of the very literal inability to communicate, to share world views, to understand. On the other hand, racism, discrimination, classism, can be viewed as factors which heavily affect the views of this community, of its residents, by the world outside of it. The issue of class more so than race becomes paramount when attempting to understand the governmental neglect which plagues the neighborhoods in question.

9.9 Ethnic tension. The conflict between the American vs. the Latin American model played out linguistically in discourse. The material manifestation of that conflict as manifested through power relationships.

Despite their common plight, racial tension tends to be high in the neighborhood. It becomes more apparent among those of different generations, in that older individuals of non-Hispanic Euro-American or East Asian origin will get a little tense when seeing a group of Hispanic or African American youths, or the way older Hispanic individuals will become tense around young African Americans. Among younger individuals, self segregation seems to be the most common way of coping with racial tensions. Perhaps the height of this manifested tension and segregation is exemplified by the police presence in the area, which can in general be seen as a metaphor for the overall relationship between Hispanic society and mainstream American culture. The police makes it clear that they are patrolling "outsiders" and the alienation which the inhabitants of this area feel from mainstream society becomes apparent through the paranoid tactics of the Las Vegas Metropolitan Police Department. While walking through the neighborhood, all it took was to talk on a cell phone for the police to pace slowly behind me in their car, staring intently, attempting to prejudge my following actions. Yet in a predominantly white, middle or upper class neighborhood, talking on a cell phone would never be viewed as suspicious behavior. As groups of youths walk by, the police regularly stop their cars and stare as if they are waiting for a crime to happen. At routine traffic stops, excessive force is used as cars are searched, backup is present, and hands rest on guns as the police officers constantly look around. Interestingly, there is very little police presence in the areas of the neighborhood which actually are crime ridden. It is ironic that high school kids are constantly harassed for standing on street corners or congregating in parks, while a block away drug deals occur in daylight in front of a supermarket. Likewise, illegal immigrants are dispersed and at times arrested for standing on the corner of Bonanza and Eastern soliciting work as trucks with gardening and construction company labels seek out cheap labor, yet those company automobiles are never stopped nor the illegal labor contractors arrested. Some of these men spend 13 to 18 hours a day seeking out work, only to perform 2 hours of labor. Along the same lines, the police do not take note of the mainly older gentlemen in expensive cars who regularly make rounds further down from the same corner soliciting sexual favors from the young men loitering there. Due to disparity, there are those who accept such interactions. The scene also brings to mind an issue seldom discussed, the plight of the homosexual seeking refuge from a "machista" society.

9.10   Alienation and dislocation.

There also seems to be very little police coordination in the ability to recognize actual gang members from those who simply imitate the style, as 14 and 16 year old boys who do not even wear the colors associated with neighborhood gangs are stopped while groups of well built 20 something year olds with gang tattoos, colors, and bandanas walk on by. A memorable moment was seeing two police officers, walking towards a group of young teens, their chests out, swaggering, hands on their holsters, and then all of a sudden things changed as a young man, around 25, dressed in light blue, with "187" tattooed on his forehead, and "MS 13" on his left bicep walked by. All of a sudden the police officers rushed to their parked vehicle and drove away shortly thereafter.

For the inhabitants of this area, such treatment from the supposed representatives of the government and people of Las Vegas only serves to reinforce the alienation which they already experience. Such observations beg the question as to why such policing approaches are not used in wealthy predominantly white neighborhoods such as Summerlin or Green Valley.

Walking through the community I was struck by the poverty, and by the slow pace of life. This was not what the notion of the United States is for most, it felt as though a poor suburb of Bogota, Mexico City, or San Salvador were transported to Las Vegas and placed in the middle of the city. I could not help but think that this portion of the city must seem like a refuge to its residents, a refuge from the fast paced world around them, from the coldness of a world which many literally cannot understand. Images of families taking leisurely walks in the early afternoon, of small children waiting for older siblings in front of their schools, teenage girls caring for younger siblings while doing the family's shopping, the elderly sitting in front of their doors watching the world go by, such views are a common part of the human landscape in this community. The closeness of the families becomes very apparent as daily life becomes a ritual centered on familial interaction.

9.11   Language alone does not have the power to change reality, merely to redefine it.

Yet the positive aspects of Hispanic cultures are not the only elements transplanted to Las Vegas. It must be understood that what is being dealt with is not Mexican, or Central American cultures per se, but rather the international culture of poverty, which changes very little from country to country, and for whose victims the plight is the same whether we discuss Turks in Cologne, Germany, Haitians in Montreal, Canada, or Mexicans in Las Vegas, U.S.A. For each group, migrating to the West does not end poverty, but merely replaces one form of poverty with another. Simply put, the transnationals in question lack the same skills to make it in foreign societies as they do in their own. With the difference being that in theory, while abroad, they have the potential to earn more than they would at home, so they perceive the present risk and sacrifice to be worth it in that once they return to their homeland, they can have a much better life with the money they earn in the West.

9.12   Marginality and alienation as both products and producers of social ailments. Contact with the culture and values of the "other" as conductive to conflict.

The presence of the negative aspects of the international culture of poverty greatly outnumber the positive elements of Hispanic culture in "Little Mexico." One of the most profound features is the presence of street gangs, disillusioned youths who struggle to fit into a world they feel has given them no opportunities, who grow up as part of a world their parents do not, perhaps cannot understand, they seek understanding among themselves, among those who have lived through the same culture of poverty. The graffiti on the walls of businesses, schools, apartment buildings, on trees, electric posts, street lamps, sidewalks, anywhere a daring youth with a can of spray paint can mark their territory, reads somewhat like a medieval tournament scroll, giving testament to the victims of the culture of urban poverty. Among the most troubling graffiti is the presence of swastikas and "SS" thunderbolts in alleys behind Hispanic owned businesses, and on apartment buildings. Other graffiti such as the Pinoy Boyz, Flip Side Pinoy, and Lao Boyz "tags" remind us of the universality of the gang problem. The most common graffiti however represents the Mexican gangs of the area, White Fence, 28th Street, Lil Locos, 18th Street, and Varrio San Chucos. With the spelling "varrio" used instead of "barrio" as a direct transplant from the Chicano gangs of Los Angeles. The epithet MS, standing for the Salvadorian gang Mara Salvatrucha is also a common presence, especially north of Owens Avenue. Yet the gang presence is felt in more ways than just graffiti, for the most part, the gang members themselves try to be inconspicuous during the day, but seem to be the reason why the streets which are bustling with activity during the day tend to become silenced once the sun sets. While the presence of Hispanic gangs in Las Vegas is a fairly new phenomenon, roots are already taking hold in that the situation greatly mirrors the familial institutionalization of gang membership so common in East Los Angeles. There is now in Las Vegas a generation of Hispanic children who are born into the gang life, whose parents are "veteranos," and whose children will most likely also continue the tradition. Along 28th Street, Owens Avenue, and the Cabana Park apartment complex on the corner of Bonanza and Eastern, it is a fairly common sight to see older gang members, those approaching their late twenties or early thirties in the company of their children. Some as young as 2 or 3 are dressed in gang colors, while 5 and 6 year olds are flashing gang signs. Children as young as 10 are putting in work for the local gangs and many are now rising in the prestige based hierarchy of street gangs based on the merits of their parents or older siblings rather than their own commitment to the gang as such. While they are not often dealt with, the linguistic repercussions of the ascent of gang culture are fairly great in that as Las Vegas Hispanic gangs are the direct product of California transplants, the already established slang, as well as Chicano speech patterns in general, are affecting and are being affected by the dialects of the Las Vegas Hispanic community.

In the same vein, an alarming trend is the omnipresence of teenage pregnancy. I believe that this trend correlates with the relatively low levels of attention given to the futures of girls in the neighborhood. It is very common to see school age girls taking care of younger siblings, helping their mothers, and running errands instead of attending school. Simply put, the girls are treated as women from the onset of puberty and therefore they behave as such.

9.13   Bilingualism.

While such an environment would not be expected to be conductive to bilingualism, it appears to be so. In my observations I have seen a pattern where the children and teens who do attend school tend to speak with each other in English, and in Spanish to their elders, while their elders attempt to speak to them in a mixture of Spanish and a varying degree of broken English, yet speak Spanish amongst each other.

9.14   Spanish as the language of ritual, while ritualistic discourse itself expresses hybridity.

Spanish alone however appears to be the language of the religious community, as there is no shortage of Apostolic and Pentecostal missionaries handing out Spanish language tracts, and the presence of makeshift prayer halls. The ceremonies themselves are held in Spanish, and differ from English language Pentecostal, revival services in that by changing the language they also change in order to accommodate a different world view. Icons of our Lady of Guadalupe, and Our Lord, Savior of the World tend to take center stage in the ceremonies as the stage is set for a unique combination of Protestant ministerial styles and Catholic symbolism.

While the symbolism of such rituals tends to blend the Hispanic and American cultural spheres, the sermons themselves are very context specific and deal with issues affecting daily life. Prayers are held for children to leave gangs, for the alleviation of poverty, misery, for heavenly redemption from this hell on Earth.

9.15   Meadows Village, scenes of
isolation and alienation.

Venturing west on Bonanza Road, I found myself peering at the dilapidated scenes around me, once middle class single story homes now on the verge of being condemned, carefully manicured although wilted lawns and pleasant splashes of color emanating from rust colored pots and carefully lined flower beds. The street scene was one of children running and playing, gang bangers soliciting near the fences of private residences and on corners, and families trekking home carrying their groceries. As the bus swooped up Bonanza Hill, the site turned to one of empty streets and apartments covered with graffiti signifying the presence of the White Fence and 21st St. street gangs. From down town, I found my way to the area commonly referred to as Meadows Village, roughly the area between Las Vegas Boulevard and I 15, and Sahara Avenue and Charleston Boulevard.

9.15.1 A historical orientation of Meadows Village.

Built in the 1950's, Meadows Village started out as a well to do neighborhood known for its at that time luxurious apartments, and celebrity residents. The Three Stooges, Frank Sinatra, Dean Martin, all stayed in the area at one time or another, as did may of the headliners and showgirls who performed in the Las Vegas casinos. As time went by and fashions changed, by the 1970's Meadows Village became a working class African American neighborhood. During the 1990's, as the Hispanic population in Las Vegas increased, Meadows Village turned into a temporary stop off point for newcomers from California. People would settle there due to the inexpensive rents, and would then decide where to move on from there. The area also acts as the arrival station for illegal immigrants from the Mexican state of Jalisco. Interestingly, it also acts as the starting point for some Bosnian and Albanian immigrants to the valley. Many of the elderly residents of the area, both European American as well as African American have spent their lives in the neighborhood and at old age found themselves financially unable to move as the neighborhood deteriorated. The implementation of the "Three Strikes You're Out" law in California created a mass exodus of street gangs, with Las Vegas being the main recipient of this populace, Meadows Village consequently found itself the preferred point of arrival for members of the 18th St. and White Fence street gangs. These gangs have firmly established themselves and today there is no question that this economically depressed area is their territory. The police sweeps aimed at keeping the sale of narcotic substances, prostitution, and homelessness off of Fremont Street have had a detrimental affect on Meadows Village as the individuals removed from Fremont Street have settled there. The intense gang presence, and lack of police presence have turned the area into a literal urban jungle.

9.15.2 Scenes of economic decay, hopelessness, delinquency, the other side of capitalism.

Walking through Meadows Village, I was first struck by the lack of economic activity, save for a few convenience stores and motels, many commercial buildings were locked, and at times boarded up. The residential areas fair no better, many of the buildings appear as though they have not been given proper attention for decades, unkept landscaping, buildings desperately in need of new paint jobs, 18th St. and White Fence graffiti covered walls which are disrupted only on occasion by skinhead graffiti, are the hallmarks of the area.

The human landscape at times seemed just as desolate. Homeless individuals roam the streets as though they were ghosts, as people walk past them without even an acknowledgement of their presence. On the other hand, prostitutes attract attention to themselves by flirting with those who pass by, at times flashing men to get their full attention. The average rate for sexual favors is $40, not coincidentally the same price as a rock of crack, which on the streets of Meadows Village is as good as hard currency. Drug deals are a common site as groups of 3 to 5 men walk up and down the streets advertising their merchandise and offering directions to local crack houses. While the majority of the residents in the area are Hispanic, this is not to imply that the criminal activity is mostly committed by Hispanics as peoples of African American and European American origin are involved in such activities as well.

9.15.3 Socio-economic aspects of alienation and marginality. Linguistic accessibility as the main boundary marker between groups.

Linguistic distance as parallel to the social distance from the prestige culture.

The high crime rate makes it rather difficult to talk with the residents of the neighborhood not involved in delinquent behaviors because they are afraid of those who do. Strangers are viewed wearily, and rumors of INS raids, or an undercover police presence spread quickly. Among the criminal element strangers are at first viewed as individuals seeking drugs or prostitutes. A rule of thumb in Meadows Village appears to be that once the sun sets, "civilians" in this war zone do not leave their homes. Even during the day, the site of children playing outdoors, or of families taking walks, is not that common. Segregation along ethnic lines however appears to be present as it is not uncommon to observe an apartment building, or sector of an apartment complex where everyone is of the same ethnicity. This is the case with most of the newly arrived immigrants from Mexico in the region. When interaction between groups does occur, it is dictated by two factors, namely ethnicity and linguistic accessibility. While in the criminal sphere, interaction between various ethnicities seems common, so long as communication is possible. Among the majority of the residents however, lives tend to be dictated along ethnic lines. For many, this is simply the product of their inability to speak English, for others it acts as a safety mechanism as they find comfort and understanding among those of their own kind, and still yet, for many it acts as a literal safety mechanism in that there is safety in numbers, a factor which carries much weight in a neighborhood such as this.

The Stupak Community Center acts as a gathering spot for cultural events in the area, and it is there that local residents seem to feel the most at ease when it comes to discussing the problems faced by their community, and open up to strangers. Those that partake in the center's activities however are a minute portion of the population at large, and even there, events tend to be divided along ethnic and linguistic lines.

9.16   The processes in Las Vegas' barrios as parallel to the processes which have already taken place in the barrios of Los Angeles.

In all, the linguistic divisions of the areas mirror the social segregation found within them. The acclaimed photojournalist Joseph Rodriguez referred to Los Angeles as a post-modern "Wild West," yet I believe that the term can be applied to Las Vegas as well in that the city presents itself as an uncontrolled and slightly scary place yet a land of dreams and beauty playing by its own rules. The conflict between the two worlds, the Spanish speaking and the English speaking exists within the context of a literal misunderstanding of those two worlds. A misunderstanding prompted by the literal inability to communicate one's world view to society effectively on one side, and the socio-economic marginalization of the population on the other side. Just as the human body reacts to a foreign presence within it by building up antibodies and attempting to rid itself of it, so too does the organism of society react to a foreign presence which it cannot, or better said is unwilling to understand and accommodate.

With their current marginalization, poverty, population growth, increasing rate of unemployment, soaring drop out rate, rise in teenage pregnancy, and violence, not just physical violence but also the violence of segregation and isolation, "Little Mexico" and Meadows Village are a powder kegs waiting to blow, social catastrophes which if not addressed will reach a level not unlike that of the Hispanic slum areas of Pico-Union or Boyle Heights in the Los Angeles area. This comparison is more than figurative as the population dynamics between Los Angeles and Las Vegas seem to parallel each other. Boyle Heights and the Pico Union area were wealthy Jewish neighborhoods in the years leading up to the Second World War and shortly after, while Compton and South Central were middle class, European American areas. Over the years, these areas came to be inhabited mostly by African Americans, and eventually an influx of Hispanics entered the area, creating a state of racial tension and self segregation as the African American community felt that its territorial integrity was being threatened. The exact same processes are occurring today in Las Vegas.

CHAPTER 10
The Interviews: An Orientation

10.0   An introduction to the interviews,
the processes involved.

The interviews were conducted within the area of "Little Mexico" described in my observations, and all consultants are residents of the aforementioned area, in locales ranging from the homes of the consultants to nearby restaurants and bars. Over a period of two months, from December 1st, 2003 through February 1st, 2004, seven individuals were interviewed. Efforts were taken to assure equitable selection of both sexes as consultants were sought in gender neutral establishments such as local restaurants, night spots, churches, and community events. Upon my setting out to do the research, it was my intent to simply gain an understanding of my consultants, to transcribe their stories within the theoretical framework that best serves to expand the current knowledge of language and identity among transnational groups. During both the interviews as well as the observation process, the use of the Spanish and English languages was determined by those with whom I have interacted as well as by my consultants. The language used was determined by their initiation and comfort levels. With the purpose of this approach being the creation of a natural flow of communication and expression, as well as for a more intimate dialogue. It also enabled me to track the role which the Spanish language has in their lives, the context which it is used to communicate, and in which circumstances it serves as a comfort zone. To determine the extent to which it serves as a political language for some, or as a means of everyday communication for others.

10.1 Factors affecting, and being affected by the interviews.

The results of these interviews were affected not only by the questions asked and the manner in which they were asked, but also by the racial affiliation, education level, class, gender, religious affiliation, political leanings, and age of the consultants as well. Another factor to keep in mind is that despite my fluidity in the Spanish language and knowledge of, and familiarity with, various Hispanic cultures, I discovered that my white skin proved to be a liability in approaching certain segments of the Hispanic population in the observed area. Namely, individuals with more pronounced Amerindian features, especially men, showed a great amount of mistrust and hesitance in even striking up conversations. Although the case was not so when it came to older individuals of Amerindian descent, even though a cordial distance was nonetheless observed. My own race, class, education level, gender, political leanings, and age, were also detrimental to not only the approaches which I took, but also to the reactions which I got from individuals, and the information they were willing to share.

Also, at certain levels of analysis, the study of behavior while one is speaking, and the behavior of those present but not engaged in talk cannot be analytically separated. Within this context, the issue of the physical setting in which the speaker performs gestures, or in which setting a speaker talks or makes an appearance before others is important as well. The physical setting, the social occasion in which language occurs is a necessary factor if one wishes to fully comprehend and describe the linguistic interaction which has taken place.

CHAPTER 11
The Consultants, an Overview

11.0   An introduction to my consultants, the basics.

In order to maintain confidentiality the consultants shall be referred to by the alphanumeric designations of A, B, C, D, E, F, G.

A is a 20 year old female born in Michoacan, Mexico but residing in Las Vegas since the age of 8. She graduated from Rancho High School, and continues to live with her family in the same neighborhood. Despite having worked as a secretary in an attorney's office for the past year, making $10.00 per hour, she is not really happy with the job and would like to continue her education as she already holds the highest level of education in her family, perhaps study psychology or elementary education. However, due to the size of her family, which consists of seven people, she feels obligated to work and help the family out, especially considering that her father is unemployed and her mother works as a maid at a Strip hotel.

While in Mexico, she did attend school and has two years worth of experience in a Spanish language institution, and one year's worth of experience with Spanish during high school. Her father is a monolingual Spanish speaker while her mother is a Spanish dominant bilingual. Her, and her siblings, three younger sisters and one older brother, ages 12, 15, 18, and 23, can be classified as English dominant bilinguals.

B is a 24 year old female, born in Las Vegas to Mexican parents. Upon completing high school she began taking courses at the Community College of Southern Nevada and continues to do so whenever she can afford it. She does not really know what she would like to study but the thought of studying alone keeps her at it. Despite being happy with her job as a receptionist at a local construction company, a job which pays $12.00 per hour due to the fact that she is bilingual, credit card debt and the nearness of family have kept her in the neighborhood. The lower rents in the area also mean that she can afford to live on her own. While having no formal education of the Spanish language, B can best be described as an English dominant bilingual.

C is an 18 year old female, born and raised in Mexico City, Mexico who has only been in Las Vegas for the past year. She lives with her brother, a poker dealer at a downtown casino, and his wife and two toddlers and soon to be newborn, all boys. She has a high school education, and would eventually like to study here, which is why her parents sent her to live with her brother who has been in Las Vegas for the past 8 years, and his family. However, currently she assists ESL courses, and works part time as a waitress for $5.00 an hour in a restaurant in the observed area. The family first moved to the community out of economic necessity and today see it serving more as a cultural comfort zone. Given her very limited English language skills, C can be described as a monolingual Spanish speaker. Her brother and his wife are both Spanish dominant bilinguals.

D is a 67 year old male, born and raised in Chihuahua, Mexico. He came to Las Vegas to live with his son's family some two years ago due to the passing away of his wife. D is an unemployed ranch hand and has a formal education up to the fourth grade, he spends his days walking through the neighborhood, chatting with people, gets together with other elderly people in a popular local restaurant twice a week, and helps take care of his son's four children while he and his wife are at work. His son is a casino porter and his daughter in law a maid. Their main reason for living in the community is a lack of resources to move else where, and that it acts as a comfort zone to live in a predominantly Hispanic area. D is a monolingual Spanish speaker. While his English speaking skills are rather limited, his son can be considered a Spanish dominant bilingual as can his daughter in law.

E is a 43 year old male from Michoacan, Mexico, who has been in Las Vegas for the past 15 years. His wife works as a line cook at a buffet in a Strip hotel, and he is currently unemployed. E has a sixth grade education and is a farmer by trade, he has found little work in Las Vegas and resorts to doing unstable odd jobs whenever the occasion arises. It has been a struggle to support their three children, two boys and one girl, aged 2, 7, and 13. Simply put, they live in the area because they cannot afford to move. E is a Spanish dominant bilingual.

F is a 21 year old female born in Needles, California to parents of Mexican descent. She has lived in Las Vegas for the past 7 years. The family moved to Las Vegas due to the perceived promise of better employment opportunities, however they found themselves not doing as well as they expected. Her mother is a buffet server, while her father is a buffet cook, both work on the Strip. F holds a high school degree and works as a help line operator for a local bank, earning $14.00 per hour. She attends classes at the Community College of Southern Nevada as well as the University of Nevada, Las Vegas and hopes to become a nurse. She lives at home due to it being less expensive than living alone, and helps take care of the family, which includes 2 younger siblings, boys aged 14 and 10, she believes it is important to stay and be a good role model for them considering the environment that they live in. Although F has had three years of high school Spanish, she and her family are monolingual English speakers.

G is a 32 year old male, born in Durango, Mexico, but having resided in Las Vegas since the age of 12. He has been living on his own since the age of 15, when his formal education stopped, and describes himself as a "veterano," or veteran gang member, a Hispanic designation with the same status implied as OG, or Original Gangster among

African-American street gang members. G lacks a high school degree, and really has no trade to speak of. He is currently unemployed and lives with other members of the same gang. He views it as his obligation to live in the neighborhood as it is in his words what he "has dedicated his life to" as it is his gang's self appropriated territory. While having assisted a Mexican school until the age of 12, G is an English dominant bilingual.

CHAPTER 12
The Interviews: Reflections, Results and Implications

12.0   Identity as grounded in culture, determined by discourse, and expressed through language.

An individual's sense of identity is more often than not grounded in their sense of cultural identity, in that sooner or later the realization that identity is not static sets in. A person realizes that they can be many things, more often than not at the same time. Depending on the situation, or even on one's mood, they can identify with being Mexican, Mexican-American, Chicano, American, Hispanic, North American, Latin American, Nevadan, Las Vegan, human. Over time, due to exposure to other individuals, other cultures, other contexts of being, of becoming, these identities become interwoven, so much that they merely become the distinct parts of a whole. Each part is expressed through the use of a language, whether that use is merely political, in that simple greetings, or cultural terms are used to reaffirm the identity of belonging to the given group, or whether it acts as a language of every day interaction. A part of an individual is expressed through Spanish words which is simply not the same as that expressed in English. This can best be compared to music, as the feelings a person has while listening to a cumbia band are different from those one has when listening to an American pop diva, so is the world of meanings different when engaged in the world of one language or the other. Language is not neutral, and particular linguistic forms mean nothing in themselves as they acquire meanings only from their specific contexts and their relationships to other such forms. It can in a word, a phrase, or a mere utterance transmit countless intended as well as unintended messages to countless readers, listeners, or viewers.

12.1   Identity as being shaped and reshaped over time by values. Language as the main identity marker.

Likewise, a person's understanding of themselves, and of others' cultural identity is shaped throughout their lives by the values and attitudes prevalent in their homes and their communities, becoming more fluid and more complex over time as one engages the broader society. While at the same time as the individual changes, so does their culture and those cultures with which they come into contact. When viewed as a marker of cultural identity, language can be viewed as a means of resistance to cultural homogenization, as even when speaking the same language, various social groups differentiate themselves by the way in which they speak. Within this context, language in a way acts as a metaphor for identity itself.

12.2 What it means to be Hispanic, conflicts and contradictions. The concept of "raza."

The question of what a Hispanic person looks like, or what a Hispanic person is, cannot be truly answered without the notion of language. Is a Hispanic person of African, European, East Asian, or Amerindian descent? Is their skin dark brown, light brown, olive, caramel colored, milky white, or pitch black? Are their lips thick or thin? Their noses long and pointy or short and flat? While the issue of race comes up when discussing what it means to be Hispanic, the notion of "raza" comes up time after time, yet the term itself refers more to language than to any physical attribute of a Hispanic "race." The use of the Spanish term politicizes identity, rather than being referred to as a "race" the Hispanic population becomes "raza," a term which inherently relates racial, and ethnic identity to the Spanish language. It serves as an abstract nationhood divorced from European nationalism. Like the term Hispanic itself, it implies multisubjectivity, a space where race is indeterminate and class classification becomes somewhat slippery.

12.3   Naturalizing power, the "other" and conflict.

With the inter-racial and inter-linguistic dynamics of that identity resting on who has power and who does not, and on the social dynamics which are played out as a result of this negotiation. Within this context, the Hispanic population represents the under privileged class within both the literal as well as the metaphorical discourse of power. For many, the role which Hispanics play in the racial/linguistic/power negotiations of the United States, is just taken as a "natural" part of being "Hispanic." It is something which is just seen as a given, and as an issue which not much thought is put into. Being portrayed as the "other" in a society where ascendance is placed on the construct of whiteness takes its toll on a population. We live in a society where those who can be classified as "white" are privileged as "human" in that "white" society claims the right to speak for the commonality of humanity, while anything which does not fit the category of "whiteness" is construed as "other" in relation to it. Thus while white is constructed as good and civil, the negative images of Hispanic society, street gangs, crime, poverty, are such a common representation that they are simply viewed as a given, and not questioned, just as having a good job and privileged life are common images associated with being white. The disparity between the images and reality however rests on the lack of communication between the two communities and the lack of knowledge which they have of each other. It appears that language then seems to define society as a whole rather than just culture.

12.4 The Spanish language as the locus of nostalgia without memory and the imagined homeland. The subsequent conflict and contradictions which arise due to a lack of knowledge of the Spanish language.

The role of the Spanish language for the consultants as a whole seems to be one of providing a comfort zone, of creating nostalgia without memory, something which is their own, and which links them to a place in which they are not the "other." Yet the contact which they have with the English speaking world, whether through work, or just the television set, or the knowledge that they are an island in an English speaking world, does influence their identity in that it creates a rupture in their image of Hispanic identity, in their emic view of the Spanish language. Code switching, the use of calques, loan translations, and broken English make them feel as though they are maladjusted individuals with linguistic deficiencies. Such structures are viewed as insisting upon incommunication, and as distancing their users from both the Hispanic as well as the Anglophone world. The users of such constructs feel as though they are alienated when they use them, since the use of calques can and does lead to embarrassment when dealing with proficient English speakers, just as broken English is, while code switching is viewed with considerable deference by proficient Spanish speakers. Despite such constructs being common, and the fact that code switching is governed by grammatical rules that require a speaker who is comfortable using both codes, individuals tend to feel a sense of belonging nowhere, not in the United States, nor in Mexico. The absence of a tangible, physical space to which one belongs creates the sentiment of a lack of a cultural space, and allows for individuals to seek comfort in nostalgia, the retreat to a physical space and time in which one finds a sense of belonging. It was Bakhtin who stated that "language, as a treasure house of images, is fundamentally chronotopic." Such a pattern follows the general trend of disadvantaged groups carving out spaces of dignity for themselves by making ethnic borders less permeable. An outcome of such actions however is that they tend to replicate and reinforce Anglophone stereotypes of Hispanics. While among Hispanics it can create a situation where a person is "different" because they do not speak Spanish, while at the same time being "different" in the Anglophone world for physically appearing different. Such aspects disrupt the dichotomy between self and other, centre and periphery, as well as give voice to the fear of culture loss and exclusion.

12.5   Legitimizing the transnational experience, making sense of the Hispanic pan-identity.

Within the context of nostalgia, the world becomes seen through green, white, and red colored glasses. While the realization that life is lived out in the physical and temporal space of the United States of America, in an Anglophone society is ever present, a conscious retreat from a culture viewed as hostile to the very core notions of Hispanic identity is made. Thus what is considered hostile tends to be viewed with hostility. The notion of Mexicanness is juxtaposed over a dichotomy where Mexico is taken to be a metaphor for Hispanic culture as a whole, and is portrayed in a constant conflict with the non-Latin American world. The 5th of May, which marks the battle of Puebla when in 1862, the Mexican army defeated a French invasion, is viewed as a symbol of a Hispanic people fighting off foreign aggression, a foreign threat to Hispanic culture, to the Spanish language. With the threat being magnified not only as one to Mexico, but to the entirety of Latin America. The Mexican struggle for independence from Spain is relegated to a lower position within the transmigrants' mythology. The reasons for this appear to be that the United States can be better compared to France than Spain simply due to the greater cultural and more importantly linguistic difference between the two nations. Thus a symbol of the Mexican struggle for sovereignty is translated as a symbol of Hispanidad, of being Hispanic, and the historical context is made sense out of as it is juxtaposed over the current cultural conflicts which mark Hispanic identity in the United States.

12.6 Mexican nationalism as the manifestation of nostalgia without memory.

At the same time, the appearance of an adherence to Mexican nationalism appears to be just that, an appearance.

It becomes nostalgia without memory as the very concepts of Mexican nationhood, political organization, economics, and history are not completely understood by the population in question, and are not addressed in inquiries dealing with the concept of Mexicanness. Instead, Mexico becomes viewed as one part of a puzzle, a unique part of a Hispanic whole, which is seen as marked by a common linguistic, and socio-economic struggle in the United States. The politics, history, economics, and every day struggles of the United States take center stage while Mexico becomes a land of extended family, beauty, where life is portrayed as ideal, the place of myth which is the only place where a true sense of belonging can really be experienced. The lack of knowledge of the grand narrative of Mexican history among the consultants is perhaps the main reason as to why it is so easy for them to accept the notion of a pan-identity as the more knowledge one has of their prospective grand narrative, the more likely they are to resist acknowledging another identity as equally valid within their given value system.

12.7 The conflict between forces of assimilation and the desire to remain Mexican.

Those who have spent a considerable time in the United States, and have breached through the linguistic and cultural barriers somewhat are similarly positioned except that they view the adoption of the dominant national ideology of the United States as the only way in which the Mexican, or Hispanic population in general, can reasonably improve their political, economic, and social positions. This position is especially strong among those of Mexican descent born in the United States, yet at the same time the view that they are Mexicans who happen to live in the United States, rather than simply "Americans" is prevalent. In general, there is however a lack of significant activist engagement in the systems of both nations on behalf of the transnational community, namely as virtually all of their socio-economic circumstances militate against this.

12.8 Mexico as the imagined homeland, and its symbolic representation of the Hispanic whole. The role of media and its discourse in shaping identity.

The notion of viewing oneself as Mexican, even perhaps while having only a few if any recollections of the nation, is upheld and promoted by the presence of Mexico which one experiences in the United States. Namely, the segregation of the Hispanic population, and the widespread presence of Spanish language media. Despite the realization that the Latin American soap operas and other television programs represent a commodified, European-centered image of Latin America, they are nonetheless viewed with a sense of nostalgia. They represent the ideal that everything is better in Mexico, the food tastes better, the people are nicer, even if one is poor, they still have their family and are home. Likewise, whether Europeanized or not, the images portrayed in the Latin American media portray Hispanic cultures within a positive light, something which the American media fails to accomplish. Despite personal or political convictions, the images on the television screen are adhered to because they offer a scenario where the Hispanic, the Mexican, leave the realm of "other," even if only symbolically, in that when one returns to daily affairs, they are relegated to dealing with the American reality once more. Interestingly, local media sources, such as the periodicals El Mundo, El Tiempo Libre, La Prensa, and Imagen figure little in the media repertoire of the consultants, although this may not be representative of the community at large. For those consultants with sufficient Spanish language skills to read the periodicals, the views varied from seeing the sources as nothing more than the personal forums of a few local businessmen, to simply being poorly written. Although they are consulted on a regular basis for news of community events and entertainment options catering specifically to a Hispanic audience.

12.9 The concept of the myth of return as legitimized through logical paradigms

Yet the notion of returning to Mexico for good is seen as an impossibility, and is met with the idea that when one's economic position is such that they will not need to work anymore, they will return, or for some, move to Mexico for the first time ever.

12.10 The portrayal of Hispanics within the discourse of mainstream culture as conductive to feelings of hostility.

At the same time, the image of how Hispanics feel that American society views them can be summed up by the word hostility. The overall impression is that white Americans of non-Hispanic descent, as well as African Americans view Hispanics with disdain. Language barriers, and the false belief that Hispanics are newcomers to the United States, with no historical roots and thus not a legitimate presence in the country, the view that street gang culture is simply Hispanic youth culture, as well as the myths that Hispanics are taking away jobs from "Americans," take tax dollars away from schools for "American" children, do not pay taxes, and are prone to illegal activities, are seen as the ways in which American society views them. A view which is supported by the criminalization of Hispanic identity in the mass media. A stereotype is the window to the unconscious, it is the way of deciphering how culture dreams of otherness. The notion of a stereotype is parallel to Dante's Virgil as the very concept can lead us into the underworld. It causes specifity and isolation, and is started by people with very little knowledge and exposure to the world outside of mainstream society and its power arrangements. The exotic becomes abnormal, turns into chaos as cruel reality replaces order and the known. It becomes an allegory for the mysterious. As all domination takes the form of administration, monotony becomes the breeding ground for rumor.

12.11 Socio-economic realities and identiy conflict.

The antagonistic situation is not helped as the realization that the dreams of becoming a Hispanic middle class are turned into the reality that they are no more than cheap labor. In turn, this turns on internal defense mechanisms within the Hispanic population, creating a sense of hostility in itself. In short, both populations, the Americans as well as Hispanics view each other ontologically, as essentially immutable objects, debating what they "are," rather than seeing what both are "becoming" due to their contact with each other.

12.12 A self awareness of being different, being viewed as the "other" leads to one seeing themselves as the "other."

The realities of every day life, of the marginality which is a part of every day life for Hispanics, seem to assure that entry into mainstream society, or better said, mainstream society's acceptance of the Hispanic population is far away from being accomplished any time soon. For many, this marginalization is omnipresent. To appear Mexican, Hispanic, to be the product of the miscegenation which occurred between the Spaniards and the Native population is something which cannot be disguised. Appearance becomes a marker which one wears every day of their lives. By "looking Hispanic" one is assumed to speak the Spanish language, and has all of the stereotypes of Hispanic automatically attached to them.

The marginality felt is then augmented by the realities of life, disillusionment with the inability to get higher paying employment, the racist backlash encountered outside of their ethnic enclaves.

When such experiences are had on an everyday level, it then becomes no wonder that a people can conceive of themselves as Mexicans, just temporarily displaced from Mexico by historical and socio-economic factors, rather than as individuals who are intrinsically linked to the nation state of the United States of America. Visits to Mexico, or having relatives from Mexico visit, investing in those relatives, as a way of maintaining an investment in Mexico, and providing for the opportunity to return provided economic security can be established, allows for the nurturing of culture, language, and religion, to have legitimacy in their world view. The maintaining of a legitimate link to the Mexican nation state provides for the accommodation of sentiments of belonging, and cultural identity which the United States fails to provide.

12.13 A lack of proficiency, as well as proficiency in the Spanish language as sources of stigma and alienation. The traumatic effects of linguicism on identity.

Among those who were born in the United States, or have spent most of their lives in the nation, the matter is complicated as they see themselves as United States citizens, who understand the norms of American society, have assisted U.S. public schools, and are not motivated by the same ties that bind transmigrants with Mexico, yet who typically lack access to all of the rights and privileges of citizenship due to their strong cultural identity. Which they see as having been imbued in them by their upbringing and the discriminatory reaction of the majority population against a non assimilated and somewhat easily identified subclass. However, for some, the inability to speak Spanish, creates a feeling of hurt, and of rootlessness. Mostly because of the fact that they identify themselves as being part of the wider Hispanic world, yet see their lack of ability to speak Spanish as standing in the way of being completely accepted by the Hispanic world. They see themselves as fully part of neither world. On one hand they are labeled as Hispanic because of their perceived ethnic phenotype, and yet their knowledge of the English language facilitates their interaction with mainstream society, exposes them to mainstream media, and influences their views on everything from politics and social issues to morality and family. While at the same time preventing them from fully experiencing the world view which the use of the Spanish language for everyday communication instills.

Incidentally, such stigma is not limited to those who are not proficient in Spanish. Among proficient Spanish speakers the same stigma is felt when among predominantly proficient English Speakers. Although assimilation, homogenization, is not looked upon in a positive light, integration is. With integration meaning the acceptance of cultural, ethnic, and linguistic difference, equal rights, and most importantly equal opportunities. The goal is to achieve a cultural solidarity which is sufficient to sustain a national existence. This desire is marked by the view that mainstream American society however does not share this set of beliefs as the population in question feels that Americans view poverty, crime, low levels of education, and marginality, as indicative of Hispanic culture as a whole or view Hispanic social ills as if they are either the norm or the natural reaction to the Hispanic predicament.

While difficult for adults, the effects of such stigma are traumatic during childhood. Children who look different from the majority, have an accent, or stick out because of their parents' origins are looked down upon as children can be cruel. Words become the mainstay of racial tension among children and the realization that phenotype is more important than citizenship when it comes to determining a sense of belonging arises at a young age. Most simply accept the racism which is dished out to them because they feel powerless to stop it. For many children, the Spanish language, which becomes a point of pride for them as adults, is seen as an embarrassment.

The effects of movements such as the English Only Movement and assimilation policies in general have been detrimental to the self esteem of Hispanic children at all levels of education. The lack of Hispanic educators in predominantly Hispanic schools has a large affect on the students' behavior and motivation to learn as there is a definite difference in the way in which non Hispanic educators relate to and view Hispanic children and in how Hispanic educators do so and vice versa. As it stands, there are students who will fail their Spanish courses on purpose simply because they do not want to be viewed as native Spanish speakers, while immigrant children, or the children of immigrants born in the United States feel embarrassed of their parents. There is a feeling that not being born here creates a sense of illegitimacy. Such feelings become the most played out during adolescence as many Hispanic teens will stay out of the sun, dye their hair, wear colored contact lenses, in an attempt to pass for European American. While a sense of resentment for their parents develops as they tend to blame their parents for coming to the United States, or bringing them here, and blame them for creating the situation responsible for the alienation which they feel. For these individuals, a sense of ethnic pride is only acceptable within the safe confines of family. Adolescence presents a crucial stage in the development of identity as it is the struggle to find a place in the world, a phase during which shared interests and personal similarities such as race, culture, and socioeconomic status form a large part in the construction of cliques and in effect for the basis for future identification and the selection of social spaces in which one feels that they belong. Rejection of the different is constantly present, as is the awareness of one's own difference in contrast to others.

12.14 The conflict associated with the transition from one language and thus world view, to another. The tensions brought about by the contact of competing cultural models.

Conflicts caused by the transition from a Spanish speaking to an English speaking world or vice versa make the notion of knowing oneself, understanding who and what one is, problematic to say the least. To most, identity is viewed as transparent, as being the product of how one is raised, as being shaped by interaction with others but not really as fluid. The main factor of having an identity rests on the notion of knowing oneself, of knowing the unique self which is seen as marking one's identity from birth till death. When the discovery of identity as being fluid enters the picture, conflict ensues because change becomes a constant, and thus knowledge of oneself as portrayed in a static state is impossible as self awareness and self consciousness take on new dimensions. When such a view of identity is coupled with the struggle of negotiating two world views, two languages, the perceived conflict becomes even greater.

Likewise, the American notion of being one thing or another, black or white, white or not white, belonging or other, interferes with the notion of mestizaje, of being mestizo. The result of such an internal conflict becomes the exaltation of one aspect of their heritage over another. Which heritage is stressed depends on the motives, the Spanish, European heritage tends to be emphasized when a certain degree of whiteness is desired, when one wishes to bridge into mainstream society. Or when mainstream society feels that it is extending a hand to the individual, and feels that by including them within the constraints of a type of "whiteness," that they are doing them an honor. The Indigenous heritage however also can be used as a position of power, in that it politicizes a legitimate presence in the territory of the United States. It allows for the emphasis of a heritage which predates that of European descended Americans. Also, Native Americans tend to be stereotyped in a better light than Hispanics.

12.15 Language as the main identity marker.

When it comes to the actual Spanish spoken, individuals feel that their mannerisms and way of speaking have not changed since arriving in the United States. While contact with Anglophone society, and with other variants of Spanish are acknowledged, the belief that these have any affect on one's own speech are absent. Likewise, the affect of the "generic" Spanish of the Spanish language media is overlooked. Emphasis is not placed on dialects, rather other speech is simply recognized as "different" and as existing independent of one's own. While stating that dialect differences are not viewed through a system of value judgments, and while stating that they are simply not an issue of importance, individuals will often use their particular dialect as a symbol emblematic of their origin. Along these lines, the speech of the Mexican is praised as it is viewed as being flowery, conductive to talkativeness, is full of extreme texture, plasticity, sensuality, and is literarily coded. The speech of the Mexican American on the other hand is seen as being crude, pragmatic, direct, and literarily simplistic. The function of language is also seen as being different to both groups, to the Mexican, conversation is viewed as a pleasure, a social event, ritual, an intellectual inquiry, a dialogue, full of irony, parody, and self-deprecating humor. To the Mexican American mind however, irony is viewed as insensitivity and harassment, as duplicity and hypocrisy. Language is instead used for play, imagining, inventing, nostalgia. At the same time, the Spanish language itself is seen as the unifier of a much larger, disparate group of people across different class, ethnic, and national backgrounds. However, with the collision of dialects present, this situation begs questions not only on how the process is occurring, whether conscious attention is being paid to it, but also on the outcome of such language contact. Language serves as a window into people's views of themselves vis-a-vis the dominant group as well as the other groups with whom they are associated, it expresses much more than simply a means of communication.

12.16 The merging of languages and dialects as the merging of identities.

The knowledge of other dialects being present, and the ability to recognize synonyms creates a situation where upon contact with others, one is constantly filling in a gap which is not really there. A person comes to know the words and uses both of them depending on the situation. Thus if such linguistic behavior is an indication of identity, a merging of dialects might be said to suggest a merging of identities.

12.17 Different value judgments placed on different languages. The inability to speak English viewed as the lack of a skill, while the inability to speak Spanish is seen as a lack of identity.

When it comes to language preference, and language use, the dominant language is not always the one most commonly used, but rather language usage depends more so on the social context. All participants in the interviews no matter what their proficiency, commented that their language of choice is Spanish. It is viewed as the language which they associate with family, close friends, and with their heritage, as an integral part of their identity. Interestingly, the use of one language or the other was seen as being beyond the control of the individual. For example, since older relatives speak no English, one is left with no choice but to attempt to communicate with broken Spanish, and by learning the very basic simple commands. Tales of wanting to speak with grandparents, and with frustration at not being able to do as they ask, or understand them are quite common. Such an approach eventually leads to a large communication gap between the generations. On the other hand, when in the midst of Anglophone society one is left with the choice of either using English, or on relying on someone to act as an interpreter. Yet while lament and the notion of cultural genocide were expressed at the inability to speak Spanish, the lack of English proficiency was viewed as a technical issue, the lack of a skill which can aid in employment possibilities. However, the lack of either language was recognized as being met with a certain social stigma.

Among monolingual Spanish speakers, the social context proves to be very limited, and as the Anglophone world is rarely if ever engaged, a certain feeling of being stifled, of being unable to experience social mobility in the simplest forms is present. One has either the choice of constantly relying on others for translation help, or is trapped in a relatively small social, economic, as well as geographical area in which to negotiate their existence.

Monolingual English speakers feel similar restraints, as they feel trapped within a world that does not fully accept them, and find themselves unable to fully enter the world into which they feel that they belong, that they want to belong to. While speaking English does allow them access to mainstream culture, its media, and allows them an opportunity to learn and understand this culture, the label of Hispanic assures that they are not entitled to the same opportunities and socio-economic privileges.

The English dominant bilingual consultants feel that they are in the same position as the monolingual Spanish speakers. While they have more experience with the English language, and are more proficient in it when it comes to prescriptive grammar and the technical aspects of the language, they feel that their accents impede their being viewed as Anglophone, as Americans. They feel that their knowledge of Spanish is more indicative of who and what they are, and how they are perceived than is their ability to speak English, and their understanding of "American" culture. However, when among conspecifics who are as proficient in English as the English dominant bilingual, the language used depends on the circumstances. Spanish tends to be used when dealing with the emotional realm, the cultural, or the political, while English is relegated to the realm of small talk or professional endeavors. While such a distribution can be accredited to the fact that a person is more comfortable discussing emotional matters in the language which they learn to feel in, their first language, a factor which perhaps also influences such choices is the censure of speaking Spanish in the work place. Likewise, the factor that the vocabulary associated with one's employment was learned in the United States, and the speaker is simply not proficient enough in Spanish to have that vocabulary play a role in this matter.

The notion of changing one's socio-economic state, or even of being accepted, integrated into society is viewed as impossible without assimilation. The prevalent notion is that if one looks like the mainstream view of what an American is, if one can fit into the conundrum of whiteness as prescribed by the ruling ideology, one can be a part of mainstream society with no problem. If a person can "pass" for a European, or better yet getting rid of their accent and passing for an American, then they are more apt to being accepted in the work environment and the community. However, if one is dark skinned, and shows traces of non-European origins, society still resists their presence.

12.18 The self as defined in contrast to the "other," the greater the contrast, the greater the sense of self.

It is within this construction of the other that the notion of Hispanic gains importance. While all consultants are quick to identify themselves as Mexicans before any other label, despite the Hispanic vs. Latino debate, the pan-identity of Latino or Hispanic is adhered to as well. Mexican is adhered to first because of the notion that a Mexican speaks a certain way, and therefore is easily identifiable, as well as the fact that this is what they view their families as being and always having been. Hispanic enters the scene as despite national differences, while in the United States, the Spanish language acts as a bond. Thus while difference is acknowledged, the difference between Spanish speakers is taken to be as a smaller one than that between them and the Anglophone world. Within this context, the Spanish language acts as a supranational binding force.

12.19 Cultural institutions uphold and promote the binding forces of group membership.

The power of this binding force is strengthened from all levels of life. From associating with relatives through get togethers, parties, attending Spanish language concerts, and patronizing Hispanic owned bars, nightclubs, and restaurants, one's connection to the Hispanic world, and Hispanic individuals can be maintained, as well as remolded and constantly recreated through contact with other individuals who thrive under the same pan-identity. Within this context, for many, the issue is not necessarily political, nor is it even a conscious decision, people simply feel that they are congregating with those with whom they are the most comfortable rather than viewing the situation as an ideological embracing or rejection of something. However, they do add that the reason for the comfort zone is the lack of acceptance, of a feeling of belonging, in the Anglophone world. Interestingly, such a refuge in the Spanish speaking world is taken even by those Hispanics who possess little or no Spanish language skills.

12.20 Insecurities arise upon presenting oneself to others as understanding rests on the ability to comprehend world views.

The way one chooses to identify themselves within and without the group tends to vary depending on the distance of the other party involved from one's own world view. Thus one may perceive themselves as Hispanic to the mainstream society, as Mexican to other Hispanics, or as Mexican-American, or of pertaining to a specific Mexican state to Mexicans. When dealing with individuals of all camps who have a rather provincial view of the world, some individuals are met with comments such as "I can't tell you are Hispanic," or "You don't look Hispanic." Some individuals become dumfounded by the sight of a Hispanic individual who does not meet their predetermined views of what a Hispanic individual should be. When such a view is taken by non-Hispanic individuals, it is viewed with irritation. However when other Hispanics make such comments, they tend to become ingrained over time, causing some individuals to become frustrated and even depressed as they come to view this as a questioning of their membership within the pan-identity. Yet when approached positively, and with an open mind, the same notion can be a source of pride in that difference within the pan-identity prevents the belief that all Hispanics are the same, and allows for a person to be Mexican, as well as Hispanic, and to have the ability to comprehend the value of understanding the differences between the various peoples and cultures of the Spanish speaking world. Among first generation immigrants specifically, the ethnic and racial hierarchies of the homeland tend to be transplanted and then become used to reconstruct pan-ethnic labels and identities. The choices made in the construction and expression of Hispanic identity are not only a product of the choices made in the United States, but also by the weight of choices made in the past.

12.21 Upon the recreation of traditional social hierarchies in newly created social spaces, language serves as a tool which perpetuates marginality.

At the same time, when dealing with transnationals, it is also important to note the way in which they feel that their conspecifics in the homeland view them. For the most part, there is the recognition that when they go to Mexico, their clothing styles give them away as North Americans. This is more so true for the younger individuals than the older ones however. For those who have lived in the United States for a considerable time, there is the notion that things at "home" have changed, that people now speak differently, that they dress differently, that they are simply no longer the same. The transnationals themselves however do not view themselves as having changed over time, nor as having adapted to new ways through culture contact. Likewise, despite experiencing socio-economic, and racial stigmatization in the United States, while in the homeland, Hispanic notions of prejudice and discrimination become attached to them. Transnationals find themselves in a position where they occupy the same position within the social hierarchy as they had before having migrated to the United States. They are not able to cross into the elite or even middle class spheres of Mexico socially, yet financially can enter a position where they can accommodate a lifestyle for themselves, or their relatives which they simply could not afford in any other circumstance. The notion of crossing borders, is a metaphor as well as a reality; when people cross so do their cultures, languages, and world views, contact is an essential aspect of any crossing. A question which thus arises is how does the concept of a pan-identity based on common linguistic, and to an extent historical and cultural heritage, and which takes those commonalities and arranges them in a dialectical opposition to the mainstream culture of the United States, affect the views of those in the homeland with whom the transnationals come into contact. As well as, how the ideals of the homeland affect

the concept of one's pan-identity upon re-crossing the border.

CHAPTER 13
Final Reflections

The place of otherness is fixed in the West as a subversion of Western metaphysics and is finally appropriated by the West as its limit-text, anti-West.
- Homi Bhabha

13.0   Among Hispanics, present day processes of becoming are intrinsically tied to the 500 year legacy of colonialism.

No group of people remains the same, over time, either we remake ourselves or allow others to remake us. Identity is far from being a static attribute, it is rather a contending arena of dynamic social relations which ultimately crystalize in a discursive label used to describe a specific group engaged in the act of becoming. Who we are and what becomes of us is a central issue for all of humanity. It is an issue which is ultimately tied to the nature and dynamics of the 500 year old social system which has engulfed us. Ultimately, the commodification of everything has to stop somewhere and the socialization of everything begin anew. The resurgence of all forms of ethnicity in the world economy is just one more self protecting mechanism of societies stripped of their social purpose, which is life itself, not profit. Ultimately, the endless accumulation of capital is not life-sustaining. One or the other will have to go. In that struggle, society must reinvent itself over and over again. From Mexican, to Hispanic, to Latin American, to American, today, to perhaps comunidad mundial, or World Community, tomorrow. A person is born, and through identity construction is in effect reborn as they struggle to find a meaningful place in the world.

13.1 A critique of prevalent views of the "other" by the prestige culture. Differences in discourse as the locus of conflict between groups.

Currently, in the United States as elsewhere, ethnic groups are studied ontologically, as objects essentially immutable in historic time, provoking endless discussions on whether they are something or the other instead of looking at what they are becoming. The globalized world is not a multicultural one, but rather one in which uniform standards are imposed by a small elite upon the rest, normally for their own economic benefit. It is a world where a fairly small number of powerful governments and corporate companies have succeeded in imposing a postmodern version of neocolonialism, without the need for military intervention as the realm of economics is their greatest weapon of mass destruction. It is a world whose standards are being reduced to the lifeless, plastic, non-caring control of computers and satellites, while the human dimension and the rights of the individual are pushed aside. It is certainly not a world without borders, but one in which some borders have become more permeable and open to trans-boundary movement, while others have remained as closed and sealed as ever before.

The class and ethnic struggles of the past have been in part the struggle between labels, names, and their sponsors. Such names and labels can be said to either contain the seeds of liberation or alienation. A sense of class is in turn transferred to the United States by Hispanic transnationals, one based on skin color, wealth, education, and the ability of tracing the family heritage. Hispanics bring with them a fluid sense of race and class, they also bring with them the class within which they were fixed in Latin America. While in theory they encounter a sense of greater social mobility in the United States, in practice they encounter a situation in which one type of poverty is exchanged for another. A greater sense of racism also develops, with Hispanics being both victims as well as perpetrators. There are racial, class, and cultural limits to social interactions, as well as limits of the self, such as temperament, emotional tendencies, and past conditioning, as one's own disposition is always projected.

13.2   Politics of language and power.

Language is the site and theme of historical action, dynamic and mobile, less an achieved synthesis of prescribed formulas than an unstable constellation of discourses. The notion of language as neutral, the naturalness of language standards, the perceived necessity of a single standard language for communication, national unity, law and order, success, and identity, that it is fixed and predominantly stable and defined by a stable cultural orientation, are the reasons why attempts to understand how multicultural communication could be possible are frustrating if even seriously addressed. With the notion of multiculturalism as understood in the discourse of officialdom as signaling the excercising of control over difference through the presentation of static models of diversity. Meanwhile in the official discourse of Latin America, binary understandings of race and identity tend to be rejected due to an ideological celebration of hybridity, while segregationist legislation, social practice, and economic hierarchies prevent any form of action to be taken. The current situation does not allow for the recognition of different reference points, imagery, traditions, literature, philosophy as accompanying different languages, and thus does not allow for competing cultural models, identities, to be expressed with equal legitimacy.

13.3   Language as the locus of meaning.

For Hispanics, English is the language used for the exchange and acquiring of things in an alien society. Spanish on the other hand is the language in which people conceive of themselves, and realize themselves in the act of speaking. Spanish is nostalgia, it offers an avenue which to use in order to save oneself from the decadence associated with modernity. English represents a dialectical opposition to Spanish, representing confrontation and assimilation.

13.4 The discursive nature of poverty.

For the majority of Hispanics in the United States, dark skin, a large family, and poverty are a social handicap. The competition for subservient jobs is high while the wages are extremely low, as surplus labor drives down wages. Most people simply accept such a situation because they feel powerless to stop it. In turn a high value is not placed on education nor the acquisition of greater skills, as dire socio-economic conditions create a situation in which the struggle for basic needs surpasses other endeavors. The nature of poverty is such that it is a trap, as nothing can be changed if people want to hold on to stability, a stable job, a stable way of life, avoiding the sacrifice of what little they do have. It is the desire for stability which causes people to accept poverty, a stable check, a stable lifestyle, the prospect that things will not get worse as long as the present conditions with which one has learned to live and cope with remain intact. Others on the other hand aspire to surpass poverty by advancing within the discourse of social and economic mobility. In reality however, the only way to truly escape poverty is to change the social situation, and the discursive realm responsible for the creation of that poverty in the first place. Likewise, the importance of economy and tradition outweigh the relevance of geopolitical borders while the market category of pop culture portrays itself as equaling acceptance. Even when acquired, citizenship is soon discovered to be a mere bureaucratic formality as phenotype and language are of greater importance when it comes to determining a sense of self, of identity and of the other.

13.5   The grip of colonialism, mental bondage as having far outlasted the socio-political institutions of colonialism.

The colonized mind is crippled by the corrosive memory of one's own captivity, a state of bondage exists in the mind even when physical bondage has disappeared as the colonized mind, and likewise body, has had its ancestral realm stolen. The struggle toward selfhood and equality requires the breaking out of the colony one is in and releasing oneself from the shackles of the colonizers world by demanding rights which no one is in any rush to freely offer. The colonizer still matters, and their role is still relevant as the colonized did not create nor cause the bondage which they continue to suffer today. The internal power imbalance and violence of history recreates itself through the hegemonic rule of the "civilized" world. The story told by the colonized differs from that told by the colonizer, the colonial drama is constantly reenacted in the lives of transnationals.

13.6 Segregation and marginality.

Segregation, whether imposed by the self or the other remains an attempt to banish the stranger or the unknown and gives a feeling of power through discourse. Yet, at the same time, it assumes that the perceived "natural order" is disrupted and will be threatened until the implied threat is gone. The exotic becomes abnormal, chaotic, as cruel reality replaces order and the known. Nonetheless, socialization with those deemed to be outsiders occurs and is negotiated and renegotiated within a context which views assimilation, albeit a superficial assimilation occurring through consumerism and tokenism, as the only legitimate outcome of that contact. Consequently, the authenticity of identity becomes viewed as being questioned by outsiders, as viewed somewhat with a sense of confusion. Such a world view based on the exclusion of the other sows the seeds of violence and humiliation as alienation itself represents the loss of self, the act of objectification. The effects of such measures on identity are many fold, notions of what an individual thinks they are, what the world has done to them, the way they prejudge how society will view them, and notions of what an individual deserves, all come into play.

13.7 Living a postcolonial existence.

Hispanics in the United States have not theorized about postcoloniality after the fact, have not learned about it from a workshop, nor did they wait for multiculturalism to enter the discourse of political correctness before they gave it a second thought, rather they have lived it since the initialization of contact and have struggled ever since to make sense of it. Dislocation, both physical and cultural, is an integral aspect of life in our world. For those of privilege, dislocation exists as a matter of choice, such as in instances where one relocates for the purpose of study or employment, yet for others it means being migrant workers, exiles, refugees, homeless individuals. While hegemony is disrupted through the flow of cultural property, as it nullifies fixed identities and the power relationships between them. Often times, this symbolic realm of resistance is the only viable form of resistance to hegemony. Difference in the official discourse of the United States is defined as deviation from Anglo-American norms. For Mexicans, the other, the different is symbolized by the very presence of the United States, and thus a dialectical opposition which legitimates the myth of Mexican homogeneity is created and serves as a defense mechanism against American cultural and economic imperialism. Retreat into the self and isolation is forced, history then becomes written in private spaces, the story is particular and carried by the individual. Likewise, the notion of truth is limited to memory, to the power of the mind and its presence in present moments. The researcher resides in the space of the oppressor and the oppressed, observing the space where contact and conflict occurs, as events reflect the atmosphere of society and the era in which they are situated.

13.8 Reflections on my work, contemplating achievements and implications for further investigations.

Looking back, I cannot help but ponder the extent to which my work enlightens, and engages the thinker. From the very start my aim has been to do just that, to provoke the reader to think about the issues which I address, and to offer a theoretical model with which to view this topic, as well as similar situations. I wanted to offer a new way of viewing an age old dilemma, and by including and heightening the attention paid to the role of language as the locus of meaning, and as an identity marker among transnational groups, by including the often ignored notion of pan-ethnicity and its role in identity formation, and by conducting my research in a place never before investigated in such a manner, I feel that I have accomplished what I set out to do.

By devising a theoretical approach which can be applied to any situation where two or more groups, with a history of prolonged contact and asymmetrical power relationships can be found, I was able to portray their voice within a format which can be used to show parallels between cultural processes throughout the world. The theoretical model which I propose in my work is as relevant for the study of Turkish transnationals in the European Union, the Angolans in the Republic of South Africa, Salvadoreans in Honduras, East Indians in the United Kingdom, Afghans in Iran, and North Africans in France, as it is for Hispanics in the United States and any other postcolonial contact situation with parallel processes at work.

The application of my theoretical model leads to the creation of a work which challenges the prevailing mannerisms of regularized thought, envisioning, and study which are dominated by the imperatives, perspectives, and ideological biases of the prestige culture. The first study of a segment of the largest transnational community in the United States in the nation's fastest growing city serves as a model for future research in its own right. Yet as I view the outcome of my fieldwork, I cannot help but see prospects for research projects which have yet to be touched upon in areas of long term study, let alone in new territory such as Las Vegas. Studies concerning the effect of contact between previously isolated dialects, and the effects of such linguistic interference upon the return to one's place of origin, the melting together of dialects within Hispanic barrios, and the bearing of such processes on identity formation may yield new insight into the discursive changes taking place within the Latin American world view once borders are crossed and recrossed. Further research into the generational difference in language ability and its affect on the traditional Hispanic family structure in the United States, and the conflicts arising when a monolingual English speaker is Hispanic in the eyes of Anglo society, and American in the eyes of Hispanics can further help understand the changing needs and concepts of self among transnationals. While a look into the conflict between Hispanics and the prestige culture in Las Vegas offers a chance to view historical processes parallel to those which have occurred in Los Angeles during the mid to late 1930's to early 1950's in action. Further significance arises from the fact that such a study was carried out in a city normally relegated to the realm of tourism, and the myth of wealth created by the facade of the Las Vegas Strip and legitimated by the city's phenomenal population growth and the construction of drones of planned communities. The work has sought to be the voice of the 300,000 inhabitants of the city whose discourse is not expressed to the world through travel brochures. The work allows for a view of life and processes of becoming, of constructing the self, through the eyes of the "other." Within the context of the applied theoretical format, it presents itself in a manner suitable for comparison with other locales in the United States where parallel historical processes have played themselves out.

13.9   Final thoughts and closing words.
Coming to terms with the "other."

Finally, my complete work offers a critique, and an alternative to the abundance of biased literature which paints a positive picture of the processes at work to assimilate Hispanics, as well as to the works which focus on the small, socio-economically upwardly mobile minority of Hispanics, while ignoring the plight of the great majority. The work is a contrast to the claims that commodification and equal access to market categories, and the fetishism and tokenism of minorities is the same as multiculturalism, equality, acceptance, and multivocality.

It is of utmost importance to note that critical thought does not submit to the commands to join in the ranks. Critical thought is centered upon the agency of human individuality and subjective intuition, rather than on received ideas and approved authority. There is a difference between the desire to gain knowledge of other peoples and times that is the result of understanding, compassion, reflection, debate, rational argument, ethical principle, careful study and analysis for their own sakes, and on the other hand knowledge that is part of an overall campaign of self affirmation. There is a profound difference between the desire to understand for the purpose of coexistence and the enlargement of horizons, and the will to dominate for the purpose of control.

In all, I present to you the discourse of a system of representations which challenge the prevailing manner in which the prestige culture of the United States comes to terms with the experience of the "other."

REFERENCES

Acuna, Adolfo. Occupied America, a History of Chicanos. Cambridge: Harper & Row. 1988.

Agnew, John. "Mapping Political Power Beyond State Boundaries: Territory, Identity, and Movement in World Politics." In Millennium: Journal of International Studies, 28. pp. 499-521. 1999.

Agnew, Johnm Stuart Corbridge. Mastering Space: Hegemony, Territory, and International Politica

Economy. London: Routledge. 1995.

Albrow, Martin. The Global Age: State and Society Beyond Modernity. Stanford: Stanford University Press. 1997.

Almaguer, Tomas. "Towards the Study of Chicano Colonialism." In Aztlan, II, Spring 1971. pp. 7-21. 1971.

Althusser, Louis. Lenin and Philosophy. New York: Monthly Review Press. 1972.

Appadurai, Arjun. ""Disjuncture and Difference in the Global Cultural Economy."" In Public Culture. Vol. 2. No. 2. pp. 1-24. 1990.

Appadurai, Arjun. Modernity at Large: Cultural Dimensions of Globalization. Minneapolis: University of Minnesota Press. 1996.

Bakhtin, Mikhail. The Dialogic Imagination. Austin: University of Texas Press. 1981.

Barrera, Mario. Race and Class in the Southwest: a Theory of Racial Inequality. Notre Dame: University of Notre Dame Press. 1978.

Barrera, Mario, Carlos Munoz, Carlos Omelas. "The Barrio as Internal Colony." In Urban Affairs Annual Review IV: Urban Politics and People. pp. 465-498. 1972.

Basch, Linda, Nina Glick Schiller, Christina Szanton Blanc. Nations Unbound: Transnational Projects, Postcolonial Predicaments, and Deterritorialized Nation States. Langhorne, Pa.: Gordon & Breach. 1994.

Baubock, Rainier. Transnational Citizenship: Membership and Rights in International Migration. Aldershot, UK: Edward Elgar Publishing Ltd. 1994.

Bhabha, Homi. "Liberalism and Minority Culture: Reflections on Cultures in Between." In Multicultural States: Rethinking Difference and Identity, David Bennett, ed., pp. 37-47 . New York: Routledge. 1998.

Bhabha, Homi. The Location of Culture. London: Routledge. 1993.

Bennett, David. "Introduction." In Multicultural States: Rethinking Difference and Identity, David Bennett, ed., pp.1-26 . New York: Routledge. 1998.

Bonilla, Frank."Ethnic Orbits: The Circulation of Capitals and Peoples." In Contemporary Marxism, 10. pp.148-165. 1985

Borjas, Jorge. "Friends or Strangers: The Impact of Immigrants on the U.S. Economy." In Journal of Economic Literature, 32, pp. 1667-1717. 1994.

Bueno, Eva. Imagination Beyond Nation: Latin American Popular Culture. Pittsburgh: University of Pittsburgh Press. 1998.

Burns, Allan. "Internal and External Identity Among Kanjobal Mayan Refugees in Florida." In Conflict,

Migration, and the Expression of Ethnicity, Nancie Gonzalez and Carolyn McCommon, eds, pp. 46-59. Boulder, Co.: Westview Press. 1989.

Castro, Janice. "Spanglish Spoken Here." In Time, 132, July 11, 1988. pp. 53. 1988.

Chakrabarty, Dipesh. "Modernity and Ethnicity in India." In Multicultural States: Rethinking Difference and Identity, David Bennett, ed., pp. 91-110 . New York: Routledge. 1998.

Chatterjee, P. The Nation and its Fragments. Princeton: Princeton University Press. 1993.

Chatterjee, P. Nationalist Thought and the Colonial World. Delhi: Oxford University Press. 1986.

Clifford, James. "Traveling Cultures." In Cultural Studies. Lawrence Grossberg, Cary Nelson, and Paula A. Treichler, eds., pp. 96-116. New York: Routledge. 1992.

Cockroft, James. Outlaws in the Promised Land, Mexican Immigrant Workers and America's Future. New York: Grove Press. 1986.

Cope, William, Mary Kalantzis. Multiliteracies: Literacy, Learning and the Design of Social Futures. London: Routledge. 2000.

Cortes, Fernando. La Evolucion de la Desigualdad del Ingreso Familiar Durante la Decada de los Ochenta. Mexico City: Centro de Estudios Sociologicos. 1993.

Delgado, Abelardo. Under the Skirt of Lady Justice. Denver: Barrio Publications. 1978.

Duran, Richard. Latino Language and Communicative Behavior. Norwood: Ablex. 1981.

Durand, Jorge. "Nuevas Regiones Migratorias." In Poblacion, Desarrollo, y Globalizacion. Rene Zenteno, ed., pp. 101-115. Mexico City: Sociedad Mexicana de Demografia-El Colegio de la Frontera Norte. 1998.

Durand, Jorge. Tres Premisas para Entender y Explicar la Migracion Mexico-Estados Unidos. Zamora: El Colegio de Michoacan. 2000.

Eagleton, Terry. "Five Types of Identity and Difference." In Multicultural States: Rethinking Difference and Identity, David Bennett, ed., pp. 48-52. New York: Routledge. 1998.

Ferguson, Russell, Martha Gever, Trinh Minh-ha, Cornel West. Out There: Marginalization and Contemporary Cultures. New York: The New Museum of Contemporary Art and M.I.T. 1990.

Fernandez, Florestan. The United States-Mexico Border: a Politico-Economic Profile. Notre Dame: University of Notre Dame Press. 1977.

Fletcher, P. La Casa de mis Suenos: Dreams of Hope in a Transnational Mexican Community. Boulder: Westview Press. 1999.

Flores, Guillermo. "Race and Culture in the Internal Colony: Keeping the Chicano in his Place." In Structures of Dependency, Frank Bonilla and Robert Girling, eds., pp. 189-223. Palo Alto: Nairobi Press. 1973.

Foucault, Michel. "The Subject and Power." In Michel Foucault: Beyond Structuralism and Hermeneutics, Hubert L. Dreyfuss and Paul Rabinow, eds., pp. 208-226. Chicago: The University of Chicago Press. 1983.

Fouron, Georges. "All in the Family: Gender, Transnational Migration, and the Nation-State." In Identities. Vol. 74. pp. 539-582. 2001.

Frow, John. "Economies of Value." In Multicultural States: Rethinking Difference and Identity, David Bennett, ed., pp. 53-68. New York: Routledge. 1998.

Gamalinda, Eric. The Empire of Memory. Manila: Anvil Publishing Inc. 1992.

Garza, Rodolfo, Gabriel Szekely. "Policy, Politics, and Emigration: Reexamining the Mexican Experience." In At the Crossroads: Mexican Migration and U.S. Policy, Frank Bean, ed., pp. 201-226. Oakland: Lanham.1997.

Gellner, E. Nations and Nationalism. Oxford: Blackwell. 1983.

Gilroy, Paul. "It Ain''t Where You're From It's Where You're At: The Dialectics of Diasporic Identification." In Third Text, Rasheed Aracaen, ed. pp. 3-16. 1991.

Gimenez, Martha. "Latino/Hispanic: Who Needs a Name? The Case Against a Standardized Terminology." In International Journal of Health Services, Vol. 19, No. 3. pp. 557-571. 1989.

Gimenez, Martha. "U.S. Ethnic Policies: Implications for Latin Americans." In Latin American Perspectives, Vol. 19, No. 4. pp. 7-17. 1992.

Giroux, Henry. "The Politics of National Identity and the Pedagogy of Multiculturalism in the USA." In Multicultural States: Rethinking Difference and Identity, David Bennett, ed., pp. 178-194. New York: Routledge. 1998.

Gledhill, John. Neoliberalism, Transnationalization and Rural Poverty: a Case Studey of Michoacan, Mexico. Oxford: Westview Press. 1995.

Gledhill, John. "The Contribution of Mexican Migration to Restructuring U.S. Capitalism: NAFTA as an Instrument of Flexible Accumulation." In Critique of Anthropology, 1 8:3. 1998.

Glick Schiller, Nina Basch, Linda Blanc-Szanton. Transnational Perspectives on Migration: Race, Class,

Ethnicity, and Nationalism Reconsidered. New York: New York Academy of Sciences. 1992.

Goldberg, David. Anatomy of Racism. Minneapolis: University of Minnesota Press. 1990.

Gonzalez, Nancie. "Conflict, Migration, and the Expression of Ethnicity: An Introduction" In Conflict, Migration, and the Expression of Ethnicity, Nancie Gonzalez and Carolyn McCommon, eds, pp. 1-10. Boulder, Co.: Westview Press. 1989.

Gracia, Jorge. Hispanic/Latino Identity. Oxford: Oxford University Press. 2000.

Gracia, Jorge, Pablo de Greiff. Hispanics/Latinos in the United States: Ethnicity, Rights, and Race. New York: Routledge. 2000.

Gruzinski, Serge. The Mestizo Mind: The Intellectual Dynamics of Colonialism and Globalization. New York: Routledge. 2002.

Guarnizo, Luis. Transnationalism from Below. New Brunswick: Transaction Publishers. 1998.

Gupta, Akhil. "Beyond "Culture": Space, Identity, and Politics of Difference." In Cultural Anthropology. pp 6-23. 1992.

Gutierrez, David. "Migration, Emergent Ethnicity, and the "Third Space": The Shifting Politics of Nationalism in Greater Mexico." In Journal of American History, September 1999. pp. 6-104. 1999.

Hagan, Jacqueline. Deciding to be Legal: a Maya Community in Houston. Philadelphia: Temple University Press. 1994.

Hall, Stuart. "Cultural Identity and Diaspora." In Identity: Community, Culture, Difference, J. Rutherford, ed., pp. 222-237. London: Lawrence & Wishart Ltd. 1990.

Hall, Stuart. "The Local and the Global: Globalization and Ethnicity." In Culture, Globalization, and the World System, Anthony King, ed., pp. 19-39. London: Macmillan. 1991.

Hall, Stuart. "Old and New Identities, Old and New Ethnicities." In Culture, Globalization,and the World System, Anthony King, ed., pp. 41-68. London: Macmillan. 1991.

Harners, Josiane, Michel Blanc. Bilinguality and Bilingualism. Cambridge: Cambridge University Press. 1989.

Heyman, Josiah. "State Effects on Labor Exploitation: The INS and Undocumented Immigrants at the Mexico-United States Border." In Critique of Anthropology, 18:3. 1998.

Jacobson, David. Rights Across Borders: Immigration and the Decline of Citizenship. Baltimore: The Johns Hopkins Press. 1996.

James, Paul. Nation Formation: Towards a Theory of Abstract Community. London: Sage. 1996.

Jameson, Fredric. Postmodernism or the Cultural Logic of Late Capitalism. Durham: Duke University Press. 1992.

Jenkins, Richard. "Rethinking Ethnicity: Identity, Categorization, and Power." In Race and Ethnicity: Comparative and Theoretical Approaches, John Stone and Rutledge Dennis, eds., pp. 59-71. Malden, Ma: Blackwell Publishers. 2003.

Joseph, May. Nomadic Identities: The Performance of Citizenship. Minneapolis: University of Minnesota Press. 1999.

Kaplan, Amy, Donald Pease.Cultures of United States Imperialism. Durham: Duke University Press. 1993.

Keaney, Michael. "The Local and the Global: The Anthropology of Globalization and Transnationalism." In Annual Review of Anthropology, 24, pp. 547-565. 1995.

Keaney, Michael. Reconceptualizing the Peasantry: Anthropology in Global Perspective. Oxford: Westview Press. 1996.

King, K.A. Language Revitalization Processes and Prospects. Clevdon, UK: Multilingual Matters Ltd. 2001.

Koundoura, Maria. "Multiculturalism or Multinationalism?" In Multicultural States: Rethinking Difference and Identity, David Bennett, ed., pp. 69-88 . New York: Routledge. 1998.

Kramsch, Claire. Language and Culture. Oxford: Oxford University Press. 2000.

Lancaster, Roger. "Skin Color, Race, and Racism in Nicaragua." In Race and Ethnicity: Comparative and Theoretical Approaches, John Stone and Rutledge Dennis, eds., pp. 99- 113. Malden, Ma: Blackwell Publishers. 2003.

Langer, Beryl. "Globalization and the Myth of Ethnic Community: Salvadorean Refugees in Multicultural Areas." In Multicultural States: Rethinking Difference and Identity, David Bennett, ed., pp. 163-177 . New York: Routledge. 1998.

Levitt, Peggy. "Transnational Villagers." In Race and Ethnicity: Comparative and Theoretical Approaches, John Stone and Rutledge Dennis, eds., pp. 260-273. Malden, Ma: Blackwell Publishers. 2003.

Lippi, Rosina. English with an Accent: Language, Ideology, and Discrimination in the United States. London: Routledge. 1997.

Lipski, John. Linguistic Aspects of Spanish-English Language Switching. Tempe: ASU Center for Latin American Studies. 1985.

Loomba, Ania. Colonialism/Postcolonialism. London: Routledge. 1998.

Lynn Doty, R. "The Double-Writing of Statecraft: Exploring State Responses to Illegal Immigration." In Alternatives, 21. pp. 171-189. 1996.

Mandel, Ruth. "Ethnicity and Identity Among Migrant Guestworkers in West Berlin." In Conflict,

Migration, and the Expression of Ethnicity, Nancie Gonzalez and Carolyn McCommon, eds, pp. 60-74. Boulder, Co.: Westview Press. 1989.

Marx, Karl, Frederick Engels. Manifesto of the Communist Party. Beijing: Foreign Language Press. 1975.

Massey, Douglas, Rafael Alarcon, Jorge Durand, Humberto Gonzalez. Return to Aztlan. Berkeley: University of California Press. 1987.

Mathieson, Susan. "Between Ethnicity and Nationhood: Shaka Day and the Struggle Over Zuluness in post-Apartheid South Africa." In Multicultural States: Rethinking Difference and Identity, David Bennett, ed., pp. 111-124 . New York: Routledge. 1998.

McBride, Peter. "Mexican Subculture Grows Beneath Colorado's Mountains." In High Country News, July 6, 1988. pp. 20. 1988.

McClintock, Anne, Amir Mufti, Ella Shohat. Dangerous Liaisons: Gender, Nation, and Postcolonial Perspectives. Minneapolis: University of Minnesota Press. 1997.

Melville, Margarita. "Hispanics: Race, Class, or Ethnicity?" In The Journal of Ethnic Studies, 16, 1, Spring pp. 67-87. 1988.

Norton, B. Identity and Language Learning. London: Longman. 2000.

Nussbaum, M. "Patriotism and Cosmopolitanism." In For Love of Country, Debating the Limits of Patriotism, J. Cohen, ed., pp. 2-20. Boston: Beacon. 1996.

Oboler, Suzanne. Ethnic Labels, Latino Lives: Identity and the Politics of Representation in the United States. Minneapolis: University of Minnesota Press. 1995.

Oommen, T.K. Citizenship, Nationality, and Ethnicity: Reconciling Competing Identities. Cambridge: Polity Press. 1997.

Ong, Aihwa. Flexible Citizenship: The Cultural Logics of Transnationality. Durham: Duke University Press. 1999.

Padilla, Felix. Latino Consciousness, The Case of Mexican Americans and Puerto Ricans in Chicago. Notre Dame: Notre Dame University Press. 1985.

Pessar, Patricia. "Women"s Political Consciousness and Empowerment in Local, National, and Transnational Contexts: Guatemalan Refugees and Returnees." In Identities, Vol. 7. pp. 461-500. 2001.

Polanyi, Karl. The Great Transformation. Beacon Hill: Beacon Press. 1957.

Portes, Alejandro."The Rise of Ethnicity: Determinants of Ethnic Perceptions among Cuban Exiles in Miami." In American Sociological Review, 49. pp. 183-197. 1984.

Preston, P.W. Political/Cultural Identity: Citizens and Nations in a Global Era. London: Penguin Books. 1997.

Quijano, Anibal. Modernidad, Identidad y Utopia en America Latina. Lima: Mosca Azul Editores. 1988.

Resnick, Melvyn. "Beyond the Ethnic Community: Spanish Language Roles and Maintenance in Miami." In International Journal of the Sociology of Language, 69. pp. 89-104. 1988.

Rouse, R. "Mexican Migration and the Social Space of Postmodernism." In Diaspora, 1:1. pp. 8- 23. 1991.

Roy, Beth. "Rioting Across Continental Divides." In Race and Ethnicity: Comparative and Theoretical Approaches, John Stone and Rutledge Dennis, eds., pp. 191-207. Malden, Ma: Blackwell Publishers. 2003.

Rumbaut, Ruben. "Assimilation and its Discontents." In Race and Ethnicity: Comparative and Theoretical Approaches, John Stone and Rutledge Dennis, eds., pp. 237-259. Malden, Ma: Blackwell Publishers. 2003.

Said, Edward. Beginnings: Intention and Method. New York: Basic Books. 1975.

Said, Edward. Culture and Imperialism. New York: Knopf. 1993.

Said, Edward. Freud and the Non-European. New York: Verso. 2003.

Said, Edward. Orientalism. New York: Pantheon Books. 1978.

Safran, William. "Diasporas in Modern Societies: Myths of Homeland and Return." In Diaspora 1:3, Winter, pp. 83-99. 1991.

Smith, Joan. Racism, Sexism, and the World System. Westport: Greenwood Press. 1988.

Stratton, Jon. "Multicultural Imagined Communities: Cultural Difference and National Identity in the USA and Australia." In Multicultural States: Rethinking Difference and Identity, David Bennett, ed., pp. 135- 164 . New York: Routledge. 1998.

Tomlinson, J. Cultural Imperialism. Baltimore: Johns Hopkins University Press. 1991.

Vincent, Joan. "Framing the Underclass." In Critique of Anthropology, 13:3. pp. 215-230. 1993.

Walker, Connor. "Beyond Reason: The Nature of the Ethnonational Bond." In Race and Ethnicity Comparative and Theoretical Approaches, John Stone and Rutledge Dennis, eds., pp. 141-152. Malden, Ma: Blackwell Publishers. 2003.

Willinsky, K. Learning to Divide the World: Education at Empire's End. Minneapolis: University of Minnesota Press. 1998.

Wolf, Eric. Europe and the People Without History. Berkeley: University of California Press. 1982.

About the Author

As a linguistic anthropologist having an extensive knowledge of psychological anthropology, cultural anthropology and political economy, I have sought to combine my professional knowledge with my love of and experience with Latin American cultures as well as a paramount interest in transnationalism/transmigration in order to create a work which I feel exhibits an exquisite intersection of a professional work and a labor of love.